"This is an absolute delight and I'm quite vexed that I didn't think of the idea, though I doubt I'd have written it up with the wit and verve that Alex has. It's a pleasure to read from start to finish and even the words I knew the origins of are explained with fresh vision and amusing anecdotes. Among old friends like Rachman, Masoch, and Mae West there are the unexpected shockers of people who gave their names to nicotine, knickers, and Listerine. Pleasingly light in tone and engagingly written, this is a very lovely and enjoyable thing."

—Chris Roberts,
author of *Heavy Words Lightly Thrown*

"It's a dirty job but someone's gotta do it. In *Tawdry Knickers*, dozens of notorious characters from history do it—give their names to the English language to enrich it with new words. Alex Novak has done a fine job of bringing them all together in one volume. Engaging reading."

—Anu Garg, founder of Wordsmith.org
and author of *A Word a Day*

Tawdry Knickers

And Other Unfortunate Ways to Be Remembered

*A Saucy and Spirited History
of Ninety Notorious
Namesakes*

Alex Novak

A Perigee Book

A PERIGEE BOOK
Published by the Penguin Group
Penguin Group (USA) Inc.
375 Hudson Street, New York, New York 10014, USA
Penguin Group (Canada), 90 Eglinton Avenue East, Suite 700, Toronto, Ontario M4P 2Y3, Canada
(a division of Pearson Penguin Canada Inc.)
Penguin Books Ltd., 80 Strand, London WC2R 0RL, England
Penguin Group Ireland, 25 St. Stephen's Green, Dublin 2, Ireland (a division of Penguin Books Ltd.)
Penguin Group (Australia), 250 Camberwell Road, Camberwell, Victoria 3124, Australia
(a division of Pearson Australia Group Pty. Ltd.)
Penguin Books India Pvt. Ltd., 11 Community Centre, Panchsheel Park, New Delhi—110 017, India
Penguin Group (NZ), 67 Apollo Drive, Rosedale, North Shore 0632, New Zealand
(a division of Pearson New Zealand Ltd.)
Penguin Books (South Africa) (Pty.) Ltd., 24 Sturdee Avenue, Rosebank, Johannesburg 2196,
South Africa

Penguin Books Ltd., Registered Offices: 80 Strand, London WC2R 0RL, England

While the author has made every effort to provide accurate telephone numbers and Internet addresses at the time of publication, neither the publisher nor the author assumes any responsibility for errors, or for changes that occur after publication. Further, the publisher does not have any control over and does not assume any responsibility for author or third-party websites or their content.

First edition: October 2010

Library of Congress Cataloging-in-Publication Data

Novak, Alex, 1974–
    Tawdry knickers and other unfortunate ways to be remembered : a saucy and spirited history of ninety notorious namesakes / Alex Novak—1st ed.
        p.   cm.
    Includes bibliographical references and index.
    ISBN 978-0-399-53619-9 (Perigee trade pbk. : alk. paper)
1. English language—Eponyms—Dictionaries.   2. English language—Etymology—Dictionaries.
3. Names, Personal—Dictionaries.   4. Biography—Dictionaries.   I. Title.
    PE1596.N68 2010
    423'.1—dc22   2010017106

PRINTED IN THE UNITED STATES OF AMERICA

10   9   8   7   6   5   4   3   2   1

Most Perigee books are available at special quantity discounts for bulk purchases for sales promotions, premiums, fund-raising, or educational use. Special books, or book excerpts, can also be created to fit specific needs. For details, write: Special Markets, Penguin Group (USA) Inc., 375 Hudson Street, New York, New York 10014.

·CONTENTS·

Most of us dream of a noteworthy legacy—our fifteen minutes of fame spread on to eternity. Luckily for some, the English language is chock-full of eponyms—proper names that have slipped into general usage as other forms of speech. Over time, the term *eponym* itself has come to refer both to the immortal individuals themselves and to the words they have spawned.

We ease the burden of the blind with the raised bumps of Louis Braille's tactile language (braille), we celebrate our winter holidays with the flowers Joel Roberts Poinsett introduced from Mexico (poinsettias), and we revel in Samuel Augustus Maverick's independent spirit (maverick). Yet while many of these historical figures live on with an etymological badge of honor, others have names that are (or should be) an inescapable and seemingly eternal embarrassment. Imagine the disappointment of having the sum total of your life reduced to sagging breasts (Astley Cooper), burned toast (Nellie Melba), or mouthwash (Joseph Lister).

I vividly remember the day, several years ago, when I discovered that the flying shell fragments that often end up maiming and killing more people than the explosion itself are named for an actual British officer.

That there could be a real person named Shrapnel seemed impossible to me. How could anyone live with such a legacy? Shrapnel seemed to me a devastating by-product of military engagement, not an invention for which someone might be proud. Yet proud he was. Henry Shrapnel was promoted for his ingenuity and secured both a military pension and etymological infamy. My curiosity piqued, I wondered how many more of these regrettable eponyms might exist. As my research began in earnest, these notorious namesakes began popping up everywhere. Boycott, Lynch (two of them!), "Tawdry," "Knickers"—all real people. More surprisingly, they sometimes appeared in pairs. Not only was Silhouette an actual French minister much loathed by his countrymen, but he was also friends with the bizarrely bouffanted Madame de Pompadour. Not only was Guillotin (and his family) forever regretful over his association with a ghastly device he neither invented nor perished by, but he was also part of the scientific committee charged with investigating the dubious hypnotic practices of Dr. Mesmer.

Sometimes the connections to other words and to other characters in history were almost too numerous to count, as in this example of facts pulled together from the life of Sam Houston (see *Houstonize*):

The whole affair was a veritable cavalcade of American frontier folklore. Davy "Killed Him a Bear When He Was Only Three" Crockett had joined Houston in his opposition to Andrew "Old Hickory" Jackson's treatment of Native Americans. Meanwhile, Francis

Scott "Star-Spangled Banner" Key was Houston's lawyer, and future president James "Napoleon of the Stump" Polk helped reduce his sentence after he was found guilty.

It seemed incumbent upon me to bring together this motley group of etymological misfits into one volume, and so *Tawdry Knickers and Other Unfortunate Ways to Be Remembered* was born to shine new light on the hilarious highs and lamentable lows of their histories.

Some are born notorious, while others have notoriety thrust upon them, and the individuals featured here fall mainly into two broad categories. The first are the truly nasty reprobates doomed to reap what they have sown, while the remainder are the decent and well-intentioned folks who have had the misfortune of being identified with something awful (or at least silly). A smattering of others fall somewhere in between, with a few still under evaluation by posterity.

The book is as much about the naughty nooks and crannies of history as it is about word origins. Each life story is a Pandora's box of cultural curiosities often connected in unexpected ways with others found within these pages. For that reason, the entries within each chapter are presented chronologically. You can follow the parade of French mistresses in "Style & Fashion," the evolution of automatic weapons in "War & Military," or the highs and lows of dieting fads in "Food & Drink." Multiple references within each story encourage you to embark on a choose-your-own adventure of etymology and world events.

The adventure is a global one, with heroes hailing from Brooklyn to Britain, from Turkey to Tasmania, and from New England to Norway. In Lewis Carroll's *Through the Looking-Glass*, the Red Queen tells Alice, "Speak in French when you can't remember the English for a thing." As such, many of the lamentable legacies presented here have sprung from foreign tongues, and fully a third of them appear in similar forms in French, German, Italian, and Spanish. We have the mesmerizers and masochists of Germany and Austria, the silhouettes and sadists of France, and the Casanovas and Ponzi schemers of Italy. Meanwhile, insofar as George Bernard Shaw once quipped that "England and America are two countries divided by a common language," we have a panoply of players from both sides of the pond whose names have trickled into our common language.

What to include in the book was simple; there is no shortage of eponyms, and their various stories have provided me with a peculiarly satisfying romp through world history. However, what to exclude from the book was far trickier. In the preface to John Farmer and W. E. Henley's turn-of-the-twentieth-century work *Slang and Its Analogues*, Farmer wrote, "The borderland between slang and the Queen's English is an ill-defined territory, the limits of which have never been clearly mapped out." To bring some authoritative heft to the proceedings, in all but three cases (*Houstonize, Cooper's ligaments*, and *brodie*) I avoided slang and jargon and focused instead on pedigreed words that appear in *Webster's*

New Universal Unabridged Dictionary, the *Oxford English Dictionary*, or *Merriam-Webster's Collegiate Dictionary*. I chose to highlight historical figures whose very names continue to be affected by their inclusion in our everyday speech, and I chose to omit names based on literary, biblical, or mythological characters—though our language would sorely miss the presence of the self-serving Mr. Diddler, the self-important Mrs. Malaprop, or the self-gratifying Onan. Likewise excluded are the heroes of history, such as Louis Braille, whose lives and legacies are interesting but not notorious.

While I have delighted in writing this book as diversionary cocktail entertainment, it should not be considered a definitive reference source. That said, I have avoided unsubstantiated barroom hearsay wherever possible, or, where rumors and urban legends stumble in, they are identified as such (see, appropriately, *crapper*). The dutiful student will find heavily annotated resources elsewhere, as there are many excellent dictionaries of eponyms and scholars of etymology in the world. Particularly useful to me were Robert Hendrickson's *Facts on File Encyclopedia of Word and Phrase Origins* and Dorothy Auchter's *Dictionary of Historical Allusions and Eponyms*, and special debts are owed to Jeffrey Kacirk's *Forgotten English* and Chris Roberts's *Heavy Words Lightly Thrown* for the inspiration they provided.

Some might ask, why another book of eponyms? In the same way that many cooks and farmers posit that we do not know enough about where our food comes from, I would argue that we know even less about where our language comes from. *Tawdry Knickers and Other Unfortunate Ways to Be Remembered* serves as an undercover tour of the etymological sausage factory. It is possible you may never speak the same way again.

CHAPTER ONE

Crime & Punishment

◁[Draconian]▷

adj. inhumanly cruel or severe; rigorous, inexorable, relentless

—*Webster's New Universal Unabridged Dictionary,*
Second Edition

People referring to company policies or social measures as "Draconian" are almost inevitably hyperbolic, as few dress codes or legal edicts could ever match the cold calculation of the original. When the Greek legislator Draco was once asked why he almost indiscriminately advocated capital punishment for all crimes, he allegedly said that he could recommend nothing less for most petty crimes and nothing more for more serious ones.

In the seventh century BC, Draco was asked to collect Athens's unwritten laws and codify an official legal code that would apply equally to everyone—a noble gesture. Unfortunately, Draco seemed to feel that one punishment should fit all crimes. In *Life of Solon*, Plutarch wrote of the code, "The man who was convicted of idleness, or who stole a cabbage or an apple, was liable to death no less than the robber of temples or the murderer." Three hundred years after Draco's death, the orator Demades still sniped that Draco's laws were "written in blood." Apparently, judges in Draco's time were a bit like the soft-spoken jailer in Monty Python's *Life of Brian* who confirmed the sentence of each prisoner: "Crucifixion? Good. Out the door, line on the left, one cross each. Next!" Luckily for the Greeks, the Draconian Code lasted only thirty years, after which the gentler and wiser Solon reserved the death penalty strictly for cases of murder.

To be fair, Draco's laws were an improvement over the status quo in many ways, which is surely what accounted for their acceptance and even wild popularity for a short time. Prior to Draco, Greece had no written constitution or laws and was a sort of Wild West of the ancient world. Criminals were subjected to mob justice, personal disagreements were settled through vendettas, and local magistrates tended to subscribe to cash-and-carry justice. The Draconian Code was physically written down on wooden tablets, made available to all (literate) citizens, and included specific descriptions of the qualifications needed to hold office. But it is still difficult to reconcile the one-execution-fits-all legal model. Draco and his Draconian measures have since been used to describe everything from cutting budgets to reforming health care to disciplining children.

In perhaps the greatest instance of ironic justice in history, Draco is believed to have been literally killed by kindness. Despite its somewhat callous specifics, Draco's code was highly preferable to the earlier, corrupt system and was enthusiastically embraced by large segments of the Athenian population. Indeed, Draco was greeted as a hero in many corners of the ancient city. Today, champion bullfighters are lauded with flowers flung into the ring, winning political candidates are showered with balloons and confetti, and certain rock stars are often pelted onstage with unsolicited racy undergarments (see also *knickers*). The tenth-century encyclopedic lexicon Suda recounts that Draco's supporters expressed their support by flinging their caps and cloaks at him when he entered the theater at Aegina.

He suffocated.

❧ Catherine wheel ❧

n. the figure of a wheel with spikes projecting from its circumference (in reference to the legend of St. Catherine's martyrdom), esp. in heraldry

v. to turn lateral summersaults (cart-wheel)

n. a window or compartment of a window of a circular form with radiating divisions or spokes

n. a kind of firework which rotates, while burning, in the manner of a wheel

—*Oxford English Dictionary*

Much of what we know of St. Catherine of Alexandria may be shrouded in myth, but for those many thousands tortured on her wooden namesake in the Middle Ages, her legacy was a grisly reality.

Originating in ancient Greece, the "breaking wheel" was a primitive but effective torture device used for nearly three thousand years for interrogation or general cruelty. In most cases, a victim would be placed on the wheel and his or her limbs would be beaten with a cudgel through the spokes. Alternatively, an executed body might simply be displayed on the wheel as a cautionary tableau. So gruesome were the torture sessions that took place (sometimes extending over days) that occasionally an executioner would deliver a deliberately lethal strike, known in French as a *coup de grâce*, or "blow of mercy." (As a linguistic aside, when *coup de grâce* is mispronounced in English—as it most commonly is, with a dropped *s* sound—the phrase becomes *coup de gras* [blow of fat] or, worse, *cou de gras* [neck of fat].)

Religious lore has it that sometime around the turn of the fourth century AD, young Catherine of Alexandria allegedly visited the Emperor of Rome, perhaps Maximinus, and went on a bit of a conversion spree. Though she could not talk the emperor into easing up on the Christians, she did manage to convince his wife and several advisers to come around to Jesus. She was sent to jail for her efforts but ended up converting both her prison escort and all of those who came to visit her. The emperor ordered her to be executed on the breaking wheel, but it shattered when she touched it. She was then martyred instead with an ax. Devout followers believe that Catherine's body was then delivered to Mount Sinai by angels and that Emperor Justinian I built a monastery there for her in the seventh century.

Over the next several hundred years, her association with the breaking wheel stuck, and the device continued to be used well into the eighteenth century. It was not banned in France, for example, until Louis XVI sensed the public disfavor with cruel and unusual punishment just prior to the French Revolution (see *guillotine*). By that time, the application of spiked wheels in heraldry or architectural design all bore Catherine's name. Even today, her namesake wheel appears in countless stained-glass windows with a spoked design. In fact, "rose windows" such as the enormous one in the Notre Dame in Paris are sometimes referred to as "Catherine windows" in honor of the martyr.

However, the most immediately recognizable of Catherine's namesakes to modern readers is likely the carefree tumbling known alternatively as "turning Catherine wheels" and "turning cartwheels." In addition, her name has also become attached to several varieties of spinning fireworks.

With a traditional feast day celebrated on November 25, St. Catherine of the Wheel is today recognized by many as the patron saint of wheelwrights, mechanics, and, of course, virgins.

◄ derrick ►

n. a contrivance or machine for hoisting or moving heavy weights

n. a hangman; hanging; the gallows

— *Oxford English Dictionary*

Originating as the word for a hangman and then his trusty gallows, this mechanical structure is named for the British executioner who invented it and has since been employed for booms, cranes, utility poles, and oil-drilling towers. But it all started with a pardoned rapist.

In 1596, British troops rampaged in the Spanish city of Cádiz after destroying the fleet in its harbor. Led by the bold and dashing Robert Devereux, second earl of Essex, the salty dogs raped and pillaged themselves silly. To be fair, they primarily pillaged, and the ones who raped were tried, convicted, and punished accordingly in proper English style. One convict, with the surname of Derrick (his first name is identified in some sources as Thomas and in others as Godfrey), was able to receive a pardon from Essex—provided he was willing to assume the position of public executioner at the notorious Tyburn gallows outside of London.

This human-resources plea bargaining was common practice at the time. Executioners were an unsavory lot, and public opinion of them was scarcely above those whom they were sending to the gallows—in fact, the intimidating hooded mask portrayed in classic folklore was to protect these civil servants from the vengeful retribution of grieving friends and family. It became extraordinarily difficult to find independent job candidates willing to endure the occupational hazards. However, with dozens of criminals being put to death every day in sixteenth-century England and the offer of a pardon available, many chose a new career over a noose.

Derrick's assignment to Tyburn was a particularly nasty one. The gallows there were the primary location for the execution of London criminals for nearly six centuries. Over the course of Derrick's career, it is estimated that he hanged or beheaded as many as three thousand convicts. To keep abreast of the volume at Tyburn, Derrick apparently developed a much larger and sturdier gallows that had a functioning lift and pulleys and was a mechanical wonder in comparison to the old rope-and-beam method. It also featured a longer rope (and drop) to ensure a quicker death—as opposed to the short-rope strangulation in vogue among Derrick's predecessors (see also *guillotine*). Even these innovations could not keep up with the pace of executions at Tyburn, however, and the "Triple Tree" became the preferred gallows, capable of hanging (as it did on one occasion in 1649) twenty-four people at once.

Derrick's name came to be associated with executioners in general, then with the elaborate gallows he invented, and finally with all manner of construction booms. Meanwhile, the great irony of Derrick's life was that despite having his own life pardoned by the Earl of Essex, it was he who ultimately swung the blade at Essex's execution for treason. In perhaps the most prescient motion-picture casting in history, Warner Brothers decided to pitch Errol Flynn (see *in like Flynn*) alongside Bette Davis as the rapist-pardoning Earl of Essex in 1939's *Private Lives of Elizabeth and Essex*. Three years later, Flynn found himself on trial and eventually exonerated of multiple charges—of statutory rape.

⊰ guillotine ⊱

> *n.* an instrument used in France (esp. during the Revolution) for beheading, consisting of a heavy knife blade sliding between grooved posts; also, execution by this instrument
>
> —*Oxford English Dictionary*

Despite *not* supporting the death penalty, *not* advocating public executions, and *not* himself dying under the blade of his namesake, Joseph-Ignace Guillotin will forever be associated with the sanguinary symbol of the French Reign of Terror.

The historical parade of torture paraphernalia would seem to support novelist Joseph Conrad's assertion that "Man is a cruel animal. His cruelty must be organized." In eighteenth-century France, popular execution methods included the breaking wheel (see *Catherine wheel*), burning at the stake, hanging, and beheading. The speed with which prisoners died usually depended on social status, with the well-to-do able to bribe executioners to sharpen their ax, and the lower classes dying of strangulation at the end of a noose or suffering multiple whacks from a dull blade.

Following the start of the French Revolution in 1789, the newly formed National Assembly decided that *"Égalité!"* applied to death row as well—that is, that all classes of condemned prisoners should be treated the same and that the death penalty need not also be the pain penalty. A crack team of consultants convened to review available options, among them surgeon Antoine Louis and professor of anatomy Joseph-Ignace Guillotin (who was also part of the committee five years earlier to decide if Franz Anton Mesmer was a blooming crackpot—see *mesmerize*). They studied existing beheading devices (including the *mannaia* of Italy, the Halifax Gibbet of England, and Morton's Maiden of Scotland) and finally designed a suitably French version, complete with an elegantly angled blade.

The prototype head-lopper was originally called a *louisette* in honor of the good surgeon Louis, but after Guillotin passionately lobbied for a more humane alternative to hanging during a debate on capital punishment, a royalist journal called *Les Actes des Apôtres* wrote and published a catchy song mocking the efforts of Guillotin (and his supporters) and asserting "his hand suddenly makes the machine that will kill us 'simply' and that we will call the Guillotine!"—thus sealing his eponymic fate. Though both Louis and Guillotin had hoped that humane (and private) executions would be the first step toward complete abolition of capital punishment, their ideals would not be realized in France for nearly two hundred more years. Instead, the newly "painless" beheadings became public spectacles in France. The scaffolds were surrounded by cheering families and *tricoteuses* (women who would knit and purl as the heads rolled). Small-scale toy models became children's playthings, and some women even wore earrings modeled after "Madame Guillotine."

During the Reign of Terror (1793–94), thousands were guillotined, including Louis XVI and Marie Antoinette. In the century that followed, its use spread around the world. Even Adolf Hitler was impressed with its speed and efficiency, and it is estimated that more than fifteen thousand German convicts lost their heads between 1933 and 1945. The last public execution by "the National Razor" in France was in 1939, but loppings continued in private through 1977, and the guillotine remained on the books as the official method of execution until the death penalty was abolished in France in 1981.

Guillotin himself died of natural causes in Paris in 1814, but his lamentable legacy with "Madame Guillotine" did not. His children spent many ensuing years unsuccessfully petitioning the French government to formally change the name of the device before eventually changing their own names instead.

❧ lynch ❧

v. to kill (an accused person) by mob action and without lawful trial, as by hanging, usually in defiance of local authority

—*Webster's New Universal Unabridged Dictionary,*
Second Edition

This word is a particularly nasty namesake, as literally dozens of people living in the United States with the last name of Lynch in the early 1800s have been put forward as its originator, leaving all with the potential for a lamentable legacy. However, two Virginia gentlemen most often rise to the top—Charles Lynch and William Lynch—each with enough irascible actions to merit consideration for ultimate notoriety. Rather than wading into the historical morass of selecting a single source, it is perhaps wiser to give both lynchers their due.

Charles Lynch was born a Quaker in Virginia in 1736 and enjoyed a patriotic career as a farmer, justice of the peace, militiaman, and Virginia senator. The close of the American Revolution during the late eighteenth century was a tense time for Anglo-American relations, and as justice of the peace in Virginia's Bedford County, Charles Lynch had to deal with plenty of sneaky limey (see *gimlet*) loyalists. Rather than shipping British defendants involved in serious crimes all the way across the state to Williamsburg for trial and risking their escape or extradition, he decided to run his own courts and carry out unsanctioned sentences of floggings, fines, and forced conscription into the American military. The Virginia General Assembly eventually decided in 1782 that his self-proclaimed "Lynch's Law" was within his rights, considering the extraordinary circumstances, and many believe that this is the definitive origin of the word.

William Lynch, meanwhile, was born six years after Charles, in 1742, and lived just a bit north, in neighboring Pittsylvania County, Virginia. With no legal background whatsoever, William Lynch and a merry band of self-described "Lynch-men" decided that vigilante justice was preferable to what they saw as the lawless free-for-all plaguing their county during the Revolutionary War and apparently signed a pact in 1780 that enjoined all members to seize and interrogate (often with a horsewhip) any alleged criminals they thought might be escaping prosecution. No less than Edgar Allan Poe immortalized the men in an 1836 editorial that included a copy of the original compact and granted them authorship of the term *lynch law*. Subsequent testimony and diaries from county residents and acquaintances supported William Lynch's claims, but scholars are still divided on whose unconstitutional shenanigans came first.

William Lynch outlived Charles by a quarter century, with the latter dying in 1796 and the former living until 1820. Scholarly indecision aside, it seems unlikely that either of them would want to be associated with the word in light of what it came to represent.

The floggings both Lynches espoused were eventually replaced by hangings, and thousands of African Americans were lynched between 1890 and 1960 in the United States, with countless more victims of all races and religions across the globe.

Perhaps future evidence will settle the etymological debate once and for all. Until then, the jury is still out, and the surname will remain an unsavory skeleton to have hanging from anyone's family tree.

⊰ burke ⊱

v. to murder (a person) in such a way as to produce no incriminating marks, usually by suffocation, and with the intention of selling the body for dissection
—*Webster's New Universal Unabridged Dictionary,*
Second Edition

This grisly eponym comes from the cursed name of William Burke, who, along with his corpse-collecting companion William Hare, became a serial murderer to generate cadavers for the students of the Edinburgh Medical College to study. Such was the state of British medicine in the 1820s.

Contrary to the twentieth-century film adaptations of Mary Shelley's classic horror story *Frankenstein* that depict the collection and assembly of assorted body parts as an essential element of the story, the original monster was a nonhuman creation of its namesake doctor (also sans the silly electric tables and sparking apparatus)—perhaps due to the fact that body snatching would have been no great shock to readers at the turn of the nineteenth century. At least in the United Kingdom, the market for fresh corpses in the early 1800s was primarily (and almost exclusively) medical schools (see also *Cooper's ligaments*), which were allowed to use only cadavers from legal executions. As capital sentences for trivial offenses (e.g., pickpocketing) were eventually outlawed (see *Draconian*), demand quickly outpaced supply—and grave robbers filled the void.

What was frighteningly commonplace at the time is almost inconceivable today. By the nineteenth century, only a few dozen individuals were executed each year in the United Kingdom, while the increasing numbers of medical students meant that many hundreds of cadavers were required. It is safe to say that at least one or two graves would have been robbed each week to satisfy the market, with each body fetching anywhere from five to twenty gold coins depending on its freshness. Coffins were soon made of iron, and relatives kept watch over new graves to ensure they stayed intact. The unfortunate side effect of these efforts was that some of the body snatchers—who came to be known, euphemistically, as "resurrectionists"—turned to murder to freshen their produce. Enter Burke and Hare.

William Burke was an Irish immigrant who left his wife and two kids to move to Edinburgh, Scotland, in 1817 and quickly picked up a mistress named Helen MacDougal. Ten years later, Burke and MacDougal moved into a boardinghouse in the West Port area of Edinburgh owned by another Irish immigrant named William Hare and his common-law wife, and the double-daters embarked on a corpses-for-cash killing spree that lasted eighteen months. In a scene straight out of Joseph Kesselring's *Arsenic and Old Lace*, the plot started out relatively innocently. An elderly tenant of the boardinghouse died naturally, and Burke and Hare sold his body to anatomist Dr. Robert Knox for use at the nearby medical college. Burke and Hare quickly discovered that they could receive double payment for particularly fresh bodies and began using intoxication and suffocation to produce a posthumous parade of sixteen more pensioners, prostitutes, and poor people that was not discovered until November 1828.

Burke and Hare and their partners were all soon arrested, but the ensuing trial proved to be an absurd affair. Of the participants in what came to be known as the West Port Murders, Hare was granted immunity for testifying against Burke, neither his wife nor Mac-Dougal could be proven to be complicit, and Dr. Knox was not prosecuted at all. Burke, on the other hand, was convicted, sentenced to death, and hanged on the twenty-eighth of January 1829. Three years later, their notoriety, as well as that of the London Burkers (see *bishop*), led to Britain's passage of the Anatomy Act of 1832, which finally curbed body snatching.

To bring the story full circle, Burke's body ended up at his adopted medical school—the Edinburgh Medical College—where it was dissected, tanned, and set up for display.

⊰ bishop ⊱

v. to murder by drowning

—*Oxford English Dictionary*

This largely antiquated word for criminal unpleasantness thankfully has no religious connection but is rather the namesake of one John Bishop, who drowned victims in a well—hanging them by their ankles—and then sold their corpses to any of a half dozen medical schools in London in the first half of the nineteenth century.

It is estimated that anatomy instructors across the United Kingdom in the 1820s required several hundred cadavers each year (see *Cooper's ligaments*), and the court system simply could not produce enough executed bodies to satisfy the need. At the same time that William Burke and William Hare were plying the wretched refuse of Edinburgh with whiskey and then suffocating them for some quick cadaver cash (see *burke*), a trio of copycat reprobates was putting its own twist on the sordid business in London. John Bishop and Thomas Williams—who, along with James May, would come to be known first as "the Resurrection Men" and later as the "London Burkers"—eventually admitted to snatching and selling more than five hundred corpses over more than a decade. But it was the murders that would put them at the end of a noose.

The Resurrection Men, perhaps after reading the murderous headlines about Burke and Hare in Edinburgh, decided to expand their cadaver business by venturing into fresh offerings, though the technique they hit upon seems somewhat unwieldy by modern sensibilities. In July 1830, the men rented a small cottage in Nova Scotia Gardens (lying in rubble below what is today the Columbia Market in London) and began luring homeless and hapless lowlifes with the promise of lodging. They then used various combinations of beer, rum, and laudanum to render their victims unconscious before lowering them—headfirst, by their ankles—into a well to drown them. Rather than suffering through the death throes, the blokes allegedly then went to their local pub for a pint or two before returning a while later to make sure nature had taken its course, and then they undressed and bagged up the bodies for delivery to various hospitals and colleges.

The Resurrection Men were finally brought to justice in November 1831, when they tried unsuccessfully to sell the body of one of their young victims to two different anatomists. Police searched the men's cottage and well, found enough suspicious clothing to elicit confessions from Bishop and Williams, and apparently made a few extra shillings themselves by charging a morbid public to tour the crime scene and carry away souvenirs. Bishop and Williams were hanged for the murders on December 5, 1831; and the public revulsion over their crimes, particularly on the heels of the arrests of Burke and Hare, led to the Anatomy Act of 1832, which provided open access to (among others) unclaimed corpses from prisons and workhouses and brought to an end the age of body snatching.

In terms of notoriety, Williams and Hare forever

played "Garfunkels" to Bishop's and Burke's "Simons." Even though all four were arrested (and, appropriately, three were eventually dissected), only the latter two names garnered entry into the dictionaries, proving, once again, that there is no free ride on the road to etymological infamy.

⊰ Ponzi scheme ⊱

n. a form of fraud in which belief in the success of a non-existent enterprise is fostered by payment of quick returns to first investors using money invested by others

—*Oxford English Dictionary*

With Bernard Madoff's multibillion-dollar swindling operation described as the largest Ponzi scheme in history, it seems appropriate to draw attention to the original Ponzi schemer—Charles Ponzi.

Born Carlo Ponzi in Italy in 1882, this natural rogue dropped out of the University of Rome in 1903 and headed to North America to make his fortune. He worked as an assistant teller in a failing Canadian bank that catered to Italian immigrants and used the money from new accounts to pay the interest payments on bad real estate loans. He later became a check forger and immigrant smuggler and spent five years in prison before finally making his way to Boston in 1917.

Always keen to find a get-rich-quick scheme, Ponzi fell upon an unglamorous but shrewd investment loophole. Nine years earlier, the 1906 Universal Postal Union congress in Rome had instituted international reply coupons (IRCs)—vouchers that could be sent to a participating foreign country in lieu of a self-addressed stamped envelope that a recipient could exchange for local postage to send a reply. Ponzi realized that American inflation after World War I resulted in postage in Italy costing far less than its equivalent in America, which meant that IRCs purchased cheaply in Italy could be cashed in for stamps in the United States, which could then be sold at a tidy profit, all perfectly legally. Of course, to make real money with the system would require millions of coupons to be purchased and traded in for millions of stamps to be sold, which Ponzi had no intention of doing. Instead, he decided to seek out a few rich saps to dupe.

Ponzi was dapper and charismatic, and his guarantee of a 50 percent return on investment in ninety days attracted enough early interest to get him rolling. He formed the Securities Exchange Company and paid back initial investors handsomely with funds from later investors, which led to a flurry of investment from regular joes hoping to beat the system. Between December 1919 and August 1920, a mere eight months, he had collected around $8 million from more than ten thousand individuals investing their life savings, mortgaging their homes, and reinvesting earlier earnings instead of cashing out. Meanwhile, Ponzi had never purchased a single coupon. What he did purchase was a mansion, a limousine, and passage for his mother to come from Italy to the land of opportunity.

There were eventually a few skeptics, including some investigators from the *Boston Post*, Clarence Barron (analyst for the financial paper *Barron's*), and a number of state officials. It was Barron who revealed that Ponzi's company would require 160 *million* postal coupons to cover all investments—while the U.S. Post Office confirmed there were only 27,000 circulating, with none being bought in serious quantities in the United States or Italy. In August 1920, federal agents raided the Securities Exchange Company and found no coupons. Ponzi was arrested, pleaded guilty to mail fraud, and spent three and a half years in federal prison before facing a nine-year state prison sentence. He quickly jumped bail; fled to Florida to set up a property scam; was deported to Italy, where he was less successful as a swindler; and finally died penniless in a Rio de Janeiro charity hospital in 1949.

The term *Ponzi scheme* is generally an American usage. Elsewhere in the world, it is almost always described as a "pyramid scheme," although there are several important differences, the most important of which is that pyramid schemes are often quite explicit in their admissions that *new* investors will be the sole source of payout for *early* investors (that is, a portion of each new investor's money is directed to earlier investors, who cash out of the system). The problem with this exponential model is that it is unsustainable, and the funds generated by new participants are soon vastly outpaced by the number of earlier investors expecting payout, at which point the system crashes.

In contrast, a true Ponzi scheme requires that the schemer be directly involved with every investor, usually under the guise of some innovative new investment approach, and there have been many, both before and after the rise and fall of its namesake. In 1880, Sarah Howe opened the bogus "Ladies Deposit" bank in Boston, promising 8 percent interest "for women only" before she vanished with the money. More than one hundred years later, in the 1990s, Louis Jay Pearlman ran an extraordinary Ponzi scheme in which he bilked more than $300 million from individuals investing in the fictitious Trans Continental Airlines (though his greater crime against humanity is surely the fact that he was the onetime manager for boy bands 'N Sync and Backstreet Boys).

Since Ponzi's day, the selling price and exchange value in stamps for international reply coupons have been adjusted to remove the potential for profit that he exploited. Regrettably, no similar regulations exist to remove the potential for profit from boy bands.

❖ Miranda ❖
(warning and rights)

adj. of, relating to, or being the legal rights of an arrested person to have an attorney and to remain silent so as to avoid self-incrimination
—*Merriam-Webster's Collegiate Dictionary, Eleventh Edition*

Despite the constitutional warm fuzzies invoked in the United States by the amendment-imbued words "You have the right to remain silent . . . ," the namesake of the pop culture cliché "Miranda warning" was an extraordinarily sad scumbag.

Ernesto Arturo Miranda was born in 1941 in Mesa, Arizona, and was a convicted criminal before finishing the eighth grade. By his eighteenth birthday, he had additionally been convicted of burglary, arrested on suspicion of armed robbery and assorted sex offenses, held in reform school for several years, and deported back to Arizona from California. A brief and dishonorably discharged stint in the army was followed by arrests and jail time for vagrancy in Texas and driving a stolen car in Tennessee before Miranda finally settled down in Arizona in the early 1960s.

In March 1963, Miranda was arrested in Phoenix and confessed (after interrogation) to the rape of an eighteen-year-old girl, and his voice was positively identified by the victim. He dutifully wrote down his confession on police stationery with printed certification on the top of each page that all statements were made "with full knowledge of my legal rights." During his trial, Miranda's court-appointed lawyer raised the objection that his client had not been informed of his constitutional rights to remain silent (and avoid self-incrimination) or to have an attorney present during his confession. The judge overruled the objections and sentenced Miranda to twenty to thirty years each for charges of rape and kidnapping.

Miranda appealed the decision to the Arizona

Supreme Court, only to have it uphold the original ruling. In 1966, the U.S. Supreme Court ultimately overturned his conviction, with Chief Justice Earl Warren insisting that the Fifth Amendment's self-incrimination clause and the Sixth Amendment's right to an attorney meant that a confession could be used as admissible evidence only if a suspect had been made aware of his rights and then waived them. Following *Miranda v. Arizona*, police across the United States were required to issue a "Miranda warning" to all criminal suspects in custody, making them aware of their constitutional rights—somewhat erroneously now identified as Miranda rights. Despite the rote treatment it gets on television cop shows, there is remarkably no single wording that has to be used for the warning as long as the gist is conveyed.

Miranda still went back to jail. His case was retried, using evidence besides his confession; he was convicted again; and he served eleven more years. He was turned down for parole four times before finally being released in 1972. He made the most of his newfound freedom and notoriety by selling autographed Miranda warning cards, getting arrested for moving violations and gun possession, working as a delivery driver, and gambling. Miranda was killed in a knife fight at a Phoenix bar in 1976 at the age of thirty-four. The prime suspect in Miranda's killing had the Miranda warning read to him from a small card, invoked his right to remain silent, and allegedly escaped to Mexico to avoid prosecution.

CHAPTER TWO

Food & Drink

◁ epicure ▷

n. one who gives himself up to sensual pleasure, esp. to eating; a glutton, sybarite

n. one who cultivates a refined taste for the pleasures of the table; one who is choice and dainty in eating and drinking

—*Oxford English Dictionary*

The Greek philosopher Epicurus would likely be horrified by the dinner-party dilettantes who invoke his name as a coat of arms for their hedonistic pursuits, and he certainly would not be swapping recipes with them at Epicurious.com. The unfortunate legacy of this peaceful thinker is a misunderstanding that has overshadowed his original beliefs for more than two thousand years.

Epicurus was born in 341 BC at the tail end of the

golden age of philosophy. Plato died seven years before he was born, and Aristotle died nineteen years after. Contrary to the modern gastronome perception, Epicurus was a model of moderation and self-control. The very inscription above the gate to his garden warned visitors that they might expect only bread and water. The philosopher took little pleasure in eating or drinking or any other physical pursuit (including sex) and taught that comfort can best be achieved through simple existence free of family and political life.

Epicurus founded the Garden School in Athens, where students ate his bread, drank his water, and shared his noble thoughts for more than two hundred years. He posted another sign at the entrance to his garden (next to his culinary warning about prison victuals), welcoming students, "Stranger, here you will do well to tarry; here our highest good is pleasure." This concept of hedonism has always been a bit of a sticky wicket, and part of the confusion of the epic of Epicurus lies in his notion of pleasure. He certainly argued that pleasure provided the happiness of life—but he had no use for sensuality. Unfortunately, over time, some of his students did. Many began buttering their daily bread, and some later toasted it into croutons on beds of arugula. Epicurus's serene and secular individualism became bastardized into wantonness and debauchery. It is only in recent memory that epicures are even considered discerning connoisseurs; for years they were merely self-gratifying slobs.

For centuries after his death, some of Epicurus's followers were equated with another gluttonous gathering of ancient Greeks—the Sybarites. Representing their own notorious namesake in the modern form of *sybarite* (notoriously luxurious), their legacy is a key descriptor in the *Oxford English Dictionary*'s definition of *epicure*. Predating Epicurus by a few hundred years, the inhabitants of the Greek colony of Sybaris in southern Italy were extraordinarily wealthy and self-indulgent. In a Grecian version of the princess and the pea, legend has it that a Sybarite was once unable to sleep because of a single rose petal under his body.

As for Epicurus, he suffered from kidney stones into his seventies. Given this diagnosis, today's holistic foodies would have approved of his love of water but would probably have warned him away from salty snacks. Calm and cheerful to the end, gentle Epicurus died in 270 BC.

⊰ grog ⊱

n. a mixture of rum and water not sweetened; hence, any kind of alcoholic drink
> —*Webster's New Universal Unabridged Dictionary,*
> *Second Edition*

It is perhaps doubly insulting to the grand and venerable Admiral Edward Vernon that his nickname "Old Grog" should come from the material of the coat he wore (grogram) and that his military legacy should be the concoction of cheap and diluted spirits used to sober up the seamen who loathed him.

Edward Vernon was born in 1684 in Westminster,

England, and rose quickly through the ranks of the British Royal Navy, achieving the rank of captain by the age of twenty-two. In his other role as a parliamentarian, he famously argued in favor of retaliation against Spain in the case of Robert Jenkins, a British mariner whose ear was cut off by a Spanish commander in 1731, leading to the—honestly—War of Jenkins' Ear waged between Britain and Spain in 1739. Vernon was eventually promoted to vice admiral and was somewhat conspicuously detested by the majority of the sailors who served under him—the notable exception being George Washington's half brother, Lawrence, who had served under the admiral in 1741 and decided to name the family estate Mount Vernon after his commander.

When strutting gallantly across the sea-swept decks, Vernon's preferred outerwear was grogram, a coarse and all-weather weave of silk, wool, and mohair often stiffened with gum. In *Good Words to You*, John Ciardi relates that Vernon further waterproofed his cloak with pitch and beeswax, which rendered it so stiff in the cold that both the grogram and the salty admiral had to be warmed by a stove to soften them—leading to the nickname of Old Grog.

Drunkenness once ran rampant on British ships as a result of spoilable fresh water being replaced first by a daily ration of a gallon of beer, then brandy, and finally a half pint of rum. To curb the inevitable alcohol-induced brawling aboard his vessels, in 1740 Old Grog declared that rum rations would henceforth be cut with water (and eventually lemon juice to improve the stagnant flavor of the water). In howling opposition, the outraged sailors quickly dubbed the unintoxicating dilution "grog," though the Royal Navy made the practice part of its official regulations in 1756, and Britain's *Dictionary of National Biography* asserted that Vernon's declaration was "perhaps the greatest improvement to discipline and efficiency ever produced by one stroke of the pen."

What Vernon's grumbling sailors did not realize at the time was that the occasional addition of citrus juice for flavor was giving them the extra vitamin C they needed to avoid scurvy; seven years later, James Lind formally proved the efficacy of citrus to curb the disease. The British Royal Navy eventually mandated a daily dose of what would become Rose's Lime Juice, the bitter flavor of which was eventually improved with the addition of gin (see *gimlet*).

Old Grog himself died in 1757, but his name lives on in word and song.

> *Well, it's all for me grog*
> *Me jolly jolly grog.*
> *It's all for me beer and tobacco.*
> *Well, I spent all me tin with the ladies drinkin' gin*
> *Far across the western ocean I must wander.*

⊲[graham cracker]⊳

n. a slightly sweet cracker made of whole wheat flour
—*Merriam-Webster's Collegiate Dictionary,*
Eleventh Edition

The innocuous brown bookends surrounding the toasted marshmallows and melted chocolate of a s'more are the namesake of one of the founders of the American vegetarian movement—Sylvester Graham. While many either associate graham crackers with the dessert course of a summer campfire feast of hot dogs and hamburgers or pour a hefty serving of milk over a breakfast bowl of Golden Grahams cereal, poor Reverend Graham is rolling over in his grave.

Graham was a nineteenth-century Presbyterian minister who was convinced that an austere diet and healthy living could help curb sexual urges—particularly "self-abuse," as he called it—as well as alcoholism. Graham was born in 1794, the seventeenth of seventeen children, and became ordained as a minister in 1826 at the peak of both a health-food craze and a temperance movement in the United States.

Though an early and ardent member of the Pennsylvania Temperance Society, Reverend Graham was, first and foremost, a crusader against lust—and he believed that bland foods were just the ticket to put out the forbidden fire. For Reverend Graham, unhealthy diets awoke excessive sexual desire, which led to disease. He once posited that ham and sausage "increase the concupiscent excitability and sensibility of the genital organs."

The Graham Diet, as it was known, was comprehensive. Fresh fruits and vegetables were okay; meat and spices were not. Only very fresh milk, cheese, and eggs could be consumed, while butter was discouraged. Modern graham crackers, which would not be named as such until nearly thirty years after his death, would have horrified Reverend Graham with their refined, bleached white flour. His original version—called Dr. Graham's Honey Biskets—called for the use of a hard, unsifted, and coarsely ground whole wheat flour called "Graham flour," which was introduced in 1829. The Graham Diet even eventually worked its way into the houses of higher learning. Oberlin College instituted such a strict version of it (abandoned in 1841) that many students opted to eat off campus, and a professor was terminated for bringing in contraband pepper to season his food.

To be sure, Graham was an early whistle-blower on some pretty reprehensible food-industry practices. He opposed the increasingly popular bakery additives of the time, such as alum and chlorine, used to make bread bake faster and appear artificially whiter. Many consumers, particularly in urban areas, regarded "refined" bread (i.e., white bread) as a more pure product. Responding to this perception, unscrupulous dairies added chalk and even plaster of paris to their milk to make it whiter. Unfortunately, Graham's rejection of meat and industrialized bread and dairy led to frequent riot threats from commercial bakers and butchers when his lectures were advertised.

But food was merely one part of a larger puritanical lifestyle. In addition to restrictions on eating, he advocated frequent bathing and hard mattresses and opposed social drinking. Zealots attended his lectures in droves, and he was famously explicit in his descriptions of despicable behavior. Women allegedly fainted when he outlined the adverse effects of masturbation.

Grahamites, as his followers were called, stayed in

Graham Boarding Houses in New York and Boston, where they abstained from alcohol, tobacco, meat, and sexy thoughts while reading his many writings—including *Lectures to Young Men on Chastity*. Among these followers were newspaperman Horace "Go West, Young Man" Greeley and Dr. John Harvey Kellogg, the inventor of cornflakes.

Reverend Graham was instrumental in founding the American Vegetarian Society in 1850, one year before his death.

Though Americans today enjoy a sweetened, less wholesome, and perhaps more lustful version of Reverend Graham's tasty namesake, it is perhaps more fitting that we remember him as Ralph Waldo Emerson dubbed him—"the poet of bran and pumpkins."

᠊᠊᠊᠊ Bantingism ᠊᠊᠊᠊

> *n.* a course of diet for reducing weight, adopted and recommended in 1864 by William Banting of London
> —*Webster's New Universal Unabridged Dictionary,*
> *Second Edition*

There was a time in London in the late nineteenth century when the question "Do you bant?" was the fashionable way to ask whether someone was trying to drop a few pounds. Such was the influence of the corpulent cabinetmaker/undertaker whose advocacy of a high-protein, low-carbohydrate diet still resonates with some weight watchers today.

Many undertakers, particularly in the 1800s, were also carpenters—coffins being the natural intersection in the Venn diagram of funerals and woodwork. William Banting was no exception, and were it not for his remarkable weight loss, he might have been remembered for little more than being a successful coffin builder for the rich and famous, most notably the Duke of Wellington. Born in 1797, by his midsixties Banting stood only five feet five inches tall but tipped the scales at more than two hundred pounds. He could not bend down to tie his own shoelaces and had to walk backward down stairs to ease the strain on his legs.

Enough was enough. After thirty years of failed weight-loss attempts, including dozens of hospital visits, starvation diets, and Turkish baths, Banting finally met with Dr. William Harvey, who ordered a strict low-carb diet. Like Dr. Salisbury (see *Salisbury steak*), Harvey believed that starch affected the body negatively and led to obesity, so gone from Banting's diet were beer, bread, and root vegetables. Harvey also opposed many sugars, so off the carpenter's shelf went sweets, milk, and butter. While man cannot live on bread alone, apparently he *can* survive on beef, mutton, fish, and sherry, which is precisely what Banting did. He lost forty-six pounds and trimmed twelve inches off his waist in one year.

At his own expense, Banting published his *Letter on Corpulence, Addressed to the Public* in 1863, in which he recommended four light but protein-rich meals a day. He rejoiced that he could still "take the most agreeable and savoury viands, meat and game pies . . . but I never, or very rarely, take a morsel of pie or pudding crusts." But the man was only human. He added, "Being fond of green peas, I take them daily in the season. . . . For this trespass I quite forgive myself." Doctors were horrified, and Banting endured a fair amount of ridicule and accusations in some corners, but his diet nonetheless became an overnight sensation, and his name became part of standard usage. Banting himself lived in comfort and health until his peaceful death in 1878, at the age of eighty-one. Though the controversial diet has always had vocal detractors, the basic concept still survives, with the most recent high-profile incarnation being a carnivore's delight—the Atkins Diet.

Though *Bantingism* does not enjoy the vogue in English of previous years, the legacy of the chunky carpenter lives on. Even today in Sweden, many people say *"Nej, tack, jag bantar"* when someone offers them something sweet. It means, "No, thank you, I am banting."

❧ Salisbury steak ❧

n. Hamburg steak
> —*Webster's New Universal Unabridged Dictionary,*
> *Second Edition*

Is it more regrettable that Dr. Salisbury's medical legacy is his chopped beefsteak namesake or that his professional recommendation was to eat it three times a day?

James Salisbury was born in New York in 1823 and worked as a chemist before becoming a physician in 1850. Like Sylvester Graham before him (see *graham cracker*), Salisbury was convinced that personal diet was the cornerstone of good health, though their theories could not have been more different. Graham was a staunch vegetarian who believed that a carnivorous diet led to lustful urges, while Salisbury was convinced that a daily beef triple-header could thwart pulmonary tuberculosis, asthma, anemia, and gout.

In addition to other battlefield horrors, Salisbury witnessed widespread diarrhea during his stint as a field doctor in the American Civil War. He eventually posited that a steady flow of coffee and ground beef was the best treatment. By 1888, he was the proponent of a full-fledged fad that called for two-thirds of one's diet to be filled with meat and claimed that too many vegetables and starch produced poisons in the digestive system that led to heart disease and even mental illness. Salisbury further advised that the beef be well-done and accompanied by hot water before and after meals.

It is curious and perhaps historically inaccurate that Dr. Salisbury is credited as the "inventor" of his namesake. By the time of his death in 1905, the minced-beef patty he was prescribing—shaped like a steak and typically served with thick gravy—had been referred to as "Hamburg steak" in many parts of the United States for decades. Meanwhile, its cousin the "hamburger"—a handheld sandwich with condiments—had come along more recently and to greater fanfare. Historians (and business owners) have several competing theories about the provenance of both, though the German city of Hamburg is indisputably the root of the words. The citizens of Hamburg, New York, claim that the first hamburger was invented and introduced by two enterprising vendors who ran out of pork at the Erie County Fair in 1885. Meanwhile, citizens of Seymour, Wisconsin, claim that "Hamburger Charlie" Nagreen invented it the same year at the Seymour Fair and named it after its related Hamburg steak (whose ultimate origin remains a mystery), then popular among Germans in the community.

For both steak and burger, the association with Germany was inescapable, and the advent of World War I and then World War II prompted some unusual patriotic revisionism and took advantage of Dr. Salisbury's convenient culinary connection. At the same time that sauerkraut became "liberty cabbage" and the German measles became "liberty measles," the hamburger became a "liberty sandwich," and the Hamburg steak officially became the Salisbury steak.

This was by no means the last time such nationalistic menu-tweaking took place. Following the Turkish invasion of Cyprus in 1974, restaurants in Greece began serving "Ellinikos kafes" (Greek coffee) instead of "Turkikos kafes" (Turkish coffee). In 2003, following French opposition to the United States' invasion of Iraq, the U.S. House of Representatives changed the menus in its cafeterias to serve "freedom fries" and "freedom toast" instead of their French counterparts. Meanwhile, the producers of French's mustard issued a press release assuring a worried public that its family name should not imply a lack of patriotism.

While the original names for hamburgers and sauerkraut have since largely returned to general usage, the Salisbury steak remains a euphemistic holdout. Today, Dr. Salisbury's prescription is an all-American icon.

❧ Fanny Adams ❧

n. tinned meat

n. stew

n. freq. prec. by *sweet*: nothing at all
— *Oxford English Dictionary*

Perhaps no one has been treated more unfairly both in her lifetime and by posterity than young Fanny Adams, who endured not only grotesque murder at the hands of a madman but also an eternity of insult added to injury at the hands of the British navy. (As an unrelated etymological aside, it would be nearly twenty years after her death before the Brits began coincidentally using the lowercased form of her first name to describe a woman's front-side unmentionables and nearly seventy years before Americans began using it to describe a woman's backside. Poor Fanny has surely suffered at the hands of the English language.)

Fanny Adams was born in 1859 in Hampshire, England. At eight years old, she was brutally murdered and dismembered by Frederick Baker, a twenty-nine-year-old clerk. Parts of her body were flung all over a hops field, and it apparently took days to piece her back together. Baker protested his innocence, but the blood on his clothes, his two blood-stained knives, and the entry in his diary that said "24th August, Saturday—killed a young girl. It was fine and hot" convinced a jury otherwise. Despite making a plea for insanity, he was publicly hanged in Winchester on Christmas Eve 1867.

Unfortunately, the indignities for poor Fanny continued two years after her death when the Royal Navy began issuing new rations of unappetizing tinned mutton. With the sailors joking that the victuals must be the chopped remains of Fanny Adams, the catchy name stuck and came to be used for all mystery meat. In time, the large tins that delivered the meat came to be called "Fannys," as did the mess kits and cooking pots used to prepare it. Believe it or not, it gets worse. The final transformation for dear Miss Adams began when sailors further adapted her name to mean "nothing at all" or the more emphatic "fuck-all." It is not uncommon to hear "sweet Fanny Adams" or, more often, the shortened "sweet F.A." cursed aboard a British vessel. Though it is principally a British phrase, it has recently made its way across the pond into American urban slang in its obscene capacity.

The more sympathetic citizens of Fanny Adams's community all pitched in on subscription to give her a proper headstone. It reads, in part, "Fear not them which kill the body but are not able to kill the soul but rather fear Him which is able to destroy both body and soul in hell." There are some in the Royal Navy, apparently unsatisfied with merely invoking Fanny's name for their rustic rations, who also refer to steak and kidney pudding as "baby's head." One can only assume that a special circle of hell awaits them.

⊰fletcherism⊱

n. the practice of chewing food slowly and thoroughly, advocated as an aid to digestion

—*Webster's New Universal Unabridged Dictionary,*
Second Edition

Illustrating that, in some cases, you are *how* you eat, the word for the nearly compulsive overchewing of food comes from Horace Fletcher, a tubby Victorian who managed to convince thousands of Americans that "Nature will castigate those who don't masticate."

Fletcher was born in 1849, smack in the middle of the nineteenth-century dieting-fad boom. In many ways like William Banting before him (see *Bantingism*), by the age of forty, Fletcher was a portly Massachusetts businessman who weighed well over two hundred pounds though standing only five and a half feet tall. He began a strict regimen of eating only when hungry and, most important, chewing every morsel of food dozens of times, so that it might be completely liquefied before being swallowed. He claimed to have lost sixty-five pounds with his simple system. Following on the heels of the puritanically vegetarian diet of the 1830s (see *graham cracker*) and the opposing meatfest of the 1860s (see *Bantingism* and *Salisbury steak*), by 1896 Fletcher was writing wildly successful dieting books and lecturing around the world and would spend the next twenty-five years as a fanatical evangelist of his own food fad.

Fletcher's concept of obsessive mastication was likely influenced by William Gladstone, the nineteenth-century British prime minister who chewed every bite of food thirty-two times and claimed that his rule of giving "every tooth of mine a chance" had brought him all of his life's success. As a bizarre marker of that success beyond his term in office, Gladstone is equally famous for trolling the midnight streets of London seeking out prostitutes to convert to Christ, resulting in the establishment of the Church Penitentiary Association for the Reclamation of Fallen Women in 1848.

As for Fletcher, he toured the world promising that his dieting technique could turn "a pitiable glutton into an intelligent epicurean" (see *epicure*). At the age of fifty-eight he trounced a cohort of college athletes in the Yale gymnasium in a series of endurance and strength tests, attributing his extraordinary health to his diet. Fletcher's gastronomical beliefs became more bizarre in his later years, as he began advising children to examine their own excretions, with no stench being a marker of good health. Toilet diving aside (see also *crapper*), his book sales and lecture appearances made him a millionaire. His food fad was embraced by a host of notables, including Thomas Edison and John D. Rockefeller. Nicknamed "the Great Masticator," Fletcher died in 1919 of bronchitis at the age of sixty-nine.

The terms *fletcherism* and *fletcherize* entered common usage within Fletcher's lifetime, but they were immortalized in his book *Fletcherism: What It Is, or How I Became Young at 60*, which was published posthumously in 1923. As is almost always the case, the fad was short-lived. Mothers inevitably tired of counting the chew clicks of children at their tables, and the novelty of compulsive self-restraint quickly wore off. However, there are still proponents of supermastication even today, who are willing to take to heart the catchy jingle made popular around the turn of the century:

> *Eat somewhat less but eat it more*
> *Would you be hearty beyond fourscore.*
> *Don't gobble your food but "Fletcherize"*
> *Each morsel you eat, if you'd be wise.*

⊰ gimlet ⊱

n. a cocktail, usually consisting of gin and lime juice
— *Oxford English Dictionary*

One widely held theory about the origin of this drink is that it was invented by Sir Thomas Gimlette of the

British Royal Navy as a way to combat scurvy. (A competing theory posits that it comes from the name of
the tool used to bore holes in the barrels of lime juice
on nineteenth-century ships.)

If you ever find yourself traveling at sea for years at
a time, it is a good idea to avoid developing scurvy.
What with the tooth and nail loss; the depression; the
skin spots, bleeding membranes, and sunken eyes;
the nonstop diarrhea; and the dying, it is in your best
interest to heal thyself. Hippocrates first described
scurvy around 400 BC. The Crusaders died from it
in the thirteenth century, as did the merchants, sailors, and other scallywags of history who spent more
time aboard ships than perishable fruits and vegetables could survive. Scurvy is caused by a deficiency of
vitamin C, whose chemical name (ascorbic acid) comes
from the Latin name for scurvy—*scorbutus*.

By the beginning of the seventeenth century, British doctors had pretty well figured out that it was the
acid from citrus fruit that scurvy-ridden sailors were
lacking. It also did not help that many undernourished
seamen were fond of eating the fat that was scrubbed
from ships' copper pans, the chemical reaction of
which prevented the absorption of vitamins. James
Cook subsequently outlawed this practice during his
circumnavigation of the globe.

As early as 1614, the surgeon general of the East
India Company recommended fresh food as a cure—
particularly oranges, lemons, and limes—and in 1747
Scottish surgeon James Lind offered formal proof that it
worked (see also *grog*). But it would take the Merchant

Shipping Act of 1867 to require all ships of the British military and merchant fleet to provide sailors with a regular dollop of lime juice—leading to the nickname "limey" for English immigrants in the early British colonies. What made this possible was a now ubiquitous cocktail mixer. By the time the act was passed, self-described "lime and lemon juice merchant" (and descendant of shipbuilders) Lauchlin Rose had patented a method for preserving citrus juice in a sugar syrup without alcohol—Rose's Lime Juice. Unfortunately, it tasted like bilgewater.

All of which leads us to the beloved Dr. Thomas Gimlette, who is believed to have joined the Royal Navy in 1879. It took him eleven years, but Gimlette finally hit on a solution for encouraging sailors to drink their daily dose of lime juice—adding gin. The now infamous surgeon *cum* mixologist was subsequently knighted and eventually retired as the British surgeon general in 1913.

The gimlet began to rise in popularity in the 1920s. It also developed an artistic cult following. Raymond Chandler allegedly revised portions of his 1954 novel *The Long Goodbye* to include mentions of the gimlet after he and his wife discovered it on a return trip from England aboard the RMS *Mauretania*. Chandler had his enigmatic private eye Philip Marlowe share a few with a war-scarred Terry Lennox in a darkened bar:

"The bartender set the drink in front of me. With the lime juice it has a sort of pale greenish yellowish misty look. I tasted it. It was both sweet and sharp at the same time."

Over the years, the gimlet has been created with varying amounts of lime juice, and today the gin is often replaced with vodka. Indeed, legendary cross-dresser and B-list movie director Ed Wood was so fond of a vodka gimlet that he spelled it backward to form his literary pseudonyms—Telmig Akdov and Akdov Telmig. But most limeys will insist (and Raymond Chandler would agree) that there's only one way to mix a proper gimlet, as Terry Lennox explains to Philip Marlowe:

"A real gimlet is half gin and half Rose's Lime Juice and nothing else. It beats martinis hollow."

⊰ mickey ⊱

n. a drink of liquor to which a powerful narcotic or purgative has been added, given to an unsuspecting person

—Webster's New Universal Unabridged Dictionary,
Second Edition

There are a few competing theories on the origins of the mickey, but the most colorful is that just a few years after Thomas Gimlette achieved fame and fortune for slipping gin into lime juice (see *gimlet*), Chicago bartender Michael Finn achieved infamy and had to close down his saloon for slipping knockout drops into his customers' drinks.

Chicago was a rough town at the turn of the twentieth century. Upton Sinclair chose the Windy City's meatpacking industry as the grittiest illustration of capitalist labor abuse in *The Jungle.* Workers needed a stiff drink, and from 1896 to 1903, the Lone Star Saloon and Palm Garden apparently served cocktails that packed a wallop. Michael "Mickey" Finn was already an unsavory character before he started managing the bar. He was a petty thief who slithered from watering hole to watering hole preying on drunken patrons. Shortly after establishing himself as the swill slinger at the Lone Star, he allegedly set up a successful racket of incapacitating customers (perhaps with chloral hydrate) and then robbing them.

Chloral hydrate was discovered in 1832 and widely used as a sedative to treat insomnia by the 1870s—even former first lady Mary Todd Lincoln took it. But what can send a person off to sleep on gossamer wings in small doses can lead to convulsions, vomiting, and even heart attacks when overdosed. Finn's victims would secretly receive a medium dose in their drink before being "escorted" from the saloon and freed of their valuables in a back alley. Finn was finally arrested in 1903, and his bar was shut down. Within a little more than a decade, even the venerable *Oxford English Dictionary* referred to any drink-delivered tranquilizer as a "Mickey Finn."

Finn's story may be apocryphal, and the term *Mickey Finn* (later, just *mickey*) has since been used to describe everything from horse laxatives to date-rape drugs. Regardless, it makes for great crime fiction and comedy fodder. In 1930, Dashiell Hammett slipped Sam Spade his first mickey in *The Maltese Falcon*, and Raymond Chandler followed suit in multiple novels with Philip Marlowe. Author P. G. Wodehouse hilariously suggested slipping a mickey into a haughty widow's bedtime Ovaltine; an animated femme fatale, Hatta Mari (see *Mata Hari*), immobilized an unsuspecting carrier pigeon with a "Mickeyblitz Finnkrieg" in a 1944 Daffy Duck short; and even *I Love Lucy* toyed with the eponym when a paranoid Lucy exclaimed "I got a mickey from Ricky!" Mickeys have appeared in James Bond films, Nancy Drew mysteries, and even a *Seinfeld* episode.

Of course, real-life encounters with chloral hydrate have not been so entertaining. Many believe that it contributed to the untimely deaths of Hank Williams, Marilyn Monroe, and Anna Nicole Smith, and it is now illegal in the United States without a prescription. As for its most infamous distributor, some accounts claim that fifteen years after his notorious trial, the original Mickey Finn was arrested again for illegally running a bar. His final cause of death is unknown.

◆ Melba toast ◆

n. bread sliced thin and dried by heat until brown and crisp

—*Webster's New Universal Unabridged Dictionary,*
Second Edition

It may be hard to believe that saying "I am Melba" once opened doors the world over, but such was the case with the grand opera diva Dame Nellie Melba in the early twentieth century. Regrettably, today it will only get you a side of burned toast.

Helen Porter Mitchell was born outside of Melbourne, Australia, in the spring of 1861. Little Nellie, as her family called her, learned to play the piano but did not even consider pursuing a musical career until adulthood. She married and had a child in 1882 and soon found a rural life in Queensland unbearable. Though she would remain married for two more decades, she abandoned her husband and two-month-old son and fled to London to be an opera star. She was twenty-one years old.

Having no luck in England, Nellie went to study in Paris with Madame Mathilde Marchesi, who quickly identified her incomparable talent, encouraged her to adopt the stage name of Melba (abbreviated from her hometown), and ushered her to stardom. The extra-ordinary soprano debuted in *Rigoletto* in Brussels in 1887 and embarked on a spectacular forty-year career, with starring roles in New York's Metropolitan Opera House, London's Covent Garden, La Scala, and the Paris Opera. She was even made a dame of the British Empire in 1918. She was a true prima donna, famous for the SILENCE! SILENCE! signs in her London dressing room; her "I am Melba!" explanations for extravagant requests; and her private train car filled with fresh caviar. So why do we associate her with desiccated bread?

While on her meteoric rise to international fame at the turn of the century, Melba often resided at the Savoy Hotel in London, where Georges Auguste Escoffier was the famed executive chef. Like many opera singers before and since, Melba was frequently concerned about her weight, and she apparently often ordered plain toast in lieu of the heavy French dishes regularly prepared. Legend has it that an assistant chef one day accidentally overtoasted a particularly thin slice of bread and sent it out to the diva, much to the horror of Escoffier. Melba loved it, began ordering it specially, and a culinary legend was born.

Melba prolonged the end of her singing career with four years of farewell concerts from 1924 to 1928, leading to the Australian expression "more farewells than Nellie Melba." She delivered her swan song in 1931, dying at the age of sixty-nine allegedly from complications following a face-lift. Headlines around the world announced her passing. Dozens of conservatories, music halls, and streets were named for her. Chef Escoffier (who adored the soprano) even named an elaborate dessert of vanilla ice cream, peaches, and raspberry sauce served betwixt the wings of a frozen swan for her (Peach Melba). But it is the inadvertent toast for which she is best remembered today.

CHAPTER THREE

War & Military

⊰[martinet]⊱

n. a rigid, inflexible, or merciless disciplinarian
— *Oxford English Dictionary*

During the Vietnam War, unpopular military officers lost to obviously hostile "friendly fire" were most often assassinated with fragmentation grenades because these nasty devices left no evidence—hence the term *fragging*. But the impulse to eliminate despised commanders dates back long before the zippy name, and one of the earliest alleged examples may be the supposedly accidental death of the unforgiving drillmaster under Louis XIV whose very name now implies uncompromising discipline.

Today, we tend to take standing armies (that is, paid, full-time soldiers, even in peacetime) for granted in modern, developed countries, but they are a relatively recent military development. Except for ancient

Rome and a few scattered examples over the next several centuries, the majority of world powers did not support standing militaries until the eighteenth century, though France's Louis XIV established an early model in 1660. Prior to his rule, states would hire mercenaries and soldiers of fortune on an as-needed basis to fight their wars, and these troops operated as independent units, with each reporting to its own commanding officer. Organizing these ragtag outfits into a cohesive army was no small task, and the Sun King tapped Jean Martinet to whip his men into shape.

Martinet was a French commoner who managed to advance through the military ranks of France and catch the attention of the monarch. He was already a lieutenant colonel and inspector general when the then twenty-two-year-old king appointed him to design all of the drills and training necessary to turn green recruits into battle-ready soldiers. Martinet was an unflinching stickler for discipline, who drilled and drilled his men into a well-oiled war machine. However, while this improved the French army, it did nothing for Martinet's popularity. Apparently, during the French siege of Duisburg in Germany in 1672, the widely loathed Martinet was "accidentally" killed by his own artillery during a charge on the city.

Still, to be fair, Martinet should be remembered for more than goose-stepping and knuckle-rapping. He was a master of efficiency and is recognized for advocating the use of storehouses and military bases to feed and support troops on the move, as opposed to the time-honored tradition of raping and pillaging. He also popularized the use of bayonets, pontoon bridges, and a type of copper assault boat—all for the greater glory of Louis XIV. Unfortunately, over the next two hundred years, most of his achievements would be forgotten by the general public, and Martinet's name would become synonymous first with military drilling and finally with unnecessarily harsh and compulsive discipline.

In an etymological twist of fate, the cat-o'-nine-tails whip used traditionally in France to discipline children is also called a "martinet," but its name is derived from the split tail of a bird, the martin (or swift). However, it is also sometimes used for sex play (see *sadism* and *masochism*), and the notion of a strict martinet meting out erotic discipline with a leather martinet is a *coïncidence extraordinaire*.

◈ shrapnel ◈

n. shell fragments scattered by any exploding shell
—*Webster's New Universal Unabridged Dictionary,*
Second Edition

War is hell. The historical trick seems to be figuring out the most unpleasant ways of unleashing that hell on your opponents. Our modern usage for the maiming detritus of an explosion actually originates with a very specific type of explosive developed by Henry

Shrapnel for the British artillery corps at the turn of the nineteenth century.

Shrapnel was an inventive British lieutenant in the Royal Artillery who was bucking for a promotion. Without a doubt, the canister shot that the British had been using since the 1400s did a pretty good job of killing people at close range. Canister shot essentially relies on the shotgun principle, in which you blast a bunch of metal balls, nails, or shards out of a muzzle and spray your enemies with hellfire. An alternative technology is the cannon, which hurls a larger ball, loaded with powder, much farther but only kills those in the immediate vicinity of its landing. Shrapnel wondered if there might be some way to marry these two widow-makers. Enter the delayed-action fuse.

In the mid-1780s, Shrapnel figured out a way to pack a projectile with all sorts of unpleasantness and have it detonate above the heads of enemy troops. Eventually his namesake became so effective that the bullets he filled his shells with became superfluous, as the shell casings themselves proved deadly enough.

The British army administrators did not embrace Shrapnel immediately. While they liked killing people, particularly at a distance, they did not come around to accepting the volatile invention until 1803, at which point Shrapnel was quickly promoted to captain, then major, and then colonel commandant. By 1814, Shrapnel had been awarded a lifetime stipend of £1,200 for his good deeds. The Duke of Wellington used Shrapnel's shells successfully to kill scores of Napoleon's soldiers during the Battle of Waterloo in 1815. Shrapnel would ultimately be promoted to major general.

After Waterloo, the world could not get enough of Shrapnel's shells. Few refinements to it were made through the course of World War I and into World War II. Even the modern cannonades of Vietnam featured the canister-shot artillery that Shrapnel had pioneered. It was not until the advent of the modern high-explosive charges that soldiers enjoy today that Shrapnel's shells faded into military history. But his name lives on in any small projectile fragments that shower a battlefield. And his invention will forever be remembered in the national anthem of the United States (written by Francis Scott Key during the terrifying British bombardment of Fort McHenry in 1814):

And the rockets' red glare, the bombs bursting in air,
Gave proof through the night that our flag was still there.

Henry Shrapnel died in 1842, presumably of natural causes.

⊰[chauvinism]⊱

n. absurd, unreasoning, and belligerent patriotism; the quality of being wildly extravagant, demonstrative, or fanatical in regard to national glory and honor *n.* unreasoning devotion to one's race, sex, etc., with contempt for other races, the opposite sex, etc.; as male *chauvinism*

—*Webster's New Universal Unabridged Dictionary,*
Second Edition

Pigs of the world, behold your namesake. The word that has become almost completely subsumed by the feminist movement is believed by many to be originally based on a French superpatriot who simply could not get enough of Napoleon.

While some modern researchers assert that his existence is a myth, the traditional theory has been that Nicolas Chauvin was a French soldier born in Rochefort toward the end of the eighteenth century. Serving initially in the First Army of the French Republic and later in Napoleon Bonaparte's Grande Armée, Chauvin was wounded seventeen times and apparently so disfigured by the end of his career that he could no longer lift his sword. (With the typical French flair for irony, Chauvin was rewarded in his retirement with a ceremonial saber.)

Chauvin received a meager military pension but nevertheless maintained nothing but love for France and, especially, the "Little Corporal." Even after Napoleon's spanking at Waterloo in 1815 and subsequent fall from favor, Chauvin maintained his infallibility. So laughable was his idolatry that he caught the attention of France's artistic community, including two playwrights, Jean and Charles Cogniard, who used him as a buffoonish character in their 1831 comedy *La cocarde tricolore* (*The Tricolor Cockade*). Other authors began using the old soldier as a caricature of fanatical patriotism as well, and his name entered the French lexicon as a synonym for bellicose nationalism.

Though English co-opted the French *chauvinisme*, it also produced its own synonym—*jingoism*. Though *jingo* (from *Jesus*) had been used as an exclamation since the seventeenth century, it was a British drinking song from the late nineteenth century that helped introduce the term *jingoism* by urging Great Britain to deter the Russian army from invading Constantinople in the Russo-Turkish War:

> *We don't want to fight, yet by Jingo if we do,*
> *We've got the ships, we've got the men,*
> *And the money, too.*

Independent British radical George Holyoake coined the term *jingoism* in a letter to the editor of the *Daily News* in 1878, and both *jingoism* and *chauvinism* were used in the United States by the turn of the twentieth century to characterize any mindless belief in partisan superiority. The latter took on its now ever-present *male* tag in the 1960s, when feminists began using the term *male chauvinism* (and, later, "male chauvinist pig") to characterize the insufferable boors espousing delusions of female inferiority.

Nicolas Chauvin would likely not know what to make of this modern application of his name, but it is probable that he would have been more horrified by the slap to the collective French face in 2003 by the jingoistic American renaming of "freedom fries" and "freedom toast" (see *Salisbury steak*). For a true patriot, some insults simply cannot stand.

⊰ Gatling gun ⊱

n. a form of machine gun, with a cluster of barrels into which the cartridges are automatically loaded at the breech

—*Oxford English Dictionary*

In one of history's great oxymoronic moments, well-intentioned doctor and inventor Richard Jordan Gatling devised his hand-cranked killing machine as a militaristic solution to the inconceivable loss of life in the American Civil War.

Gatling was a Southerner born in North Carolina in 1818 to a farmer and inventor. He initially followed in his father's footsteps and developed a seed planter, grain drill, and shovel plow before earning a medical degree in 1850. Gatling moved north to Indianapolis to practice medicine but never strayed far from inventing. It was while watching returning Civil War soldiers die more often from battlefield illnesses than gunshot wounds that he decided to work on a hyperefficient weapon.

Gatling was not so much a pacifist as a pragmatist. He did not seek to end wars, only to reduce the number of soldiers it took to fight them. Gatling wrote, "It occurred to me that if I could invent a machine—a gun—which could by its rapidity of fire, enable one man to do as much battle duty as a hundred, that it would, to a large extent, supersede the necessity of large armies, and consequently, exposure to battle and disease [would] be greatly diminished." Sadly, this proved not to be the case, and Gatling had succeeded only in creating a precursor to the modern machine gun, which has been responsible for countless deaths in the past century (see also *tommy gun* and *AK-47*).

Individual reloading during the Civil War was a time-consuming process. The Gatling gun featured multiple rifle barrels mounted around a crankable shaft, so one gunner could fire as many as four hundred rounds per minute and pick off countless unlucky single-shooters at a range of up to twenty football fields. There were many eponymous machine guns invented during the Civil War (e.g., the Gorgas, the Ripley, the Claxon, and the Williams), some of which also featured rotators and multiple barrels to avoid overheating, but only the Gatling had a foolproof, gravity-fed reloader that meant it could be operated by anyone.

Gatling's gun was perfected by 1862, but Union forces did not buy any great number until 1866, after the war's end. Gatling sold his gun patents to Colt in 1870 but remained president of the Gatling Gun Company for nearly twenty years as he pursued other invention patents, including an "Apparatus for Cleansing Wool" in 1892 and a "Flushing Apparatus for Water Closets" in 1901 (see also *crapper*). Even in the final days before his death in 1903, he was working on a patent for a type of tractor that he called a steam-powered "motor plow."

Though no one speaks of true Gatling guns being used anymore, the doctor's legacy has been preserved in a shortened slang form first used by the criminal underworld at the turn of the twentieth century and more recently by urban rappers—the gat.

⊰ tommy gun ⊱

n. a Thompson submachine gun

n. loosely, any machine gun
— *Webster's New Universal Unabridged Dictionary,*
Second Edition

The 1920s provided dark fodder for the introduction of new words into our lexicon. The gangster era "hijacked" us, took us "for a ride," and served us "bathtub gin." But the "gun that made the twenties roar" was the invention of a World War I general and one-time bovine executioner who wanted a compact "trench sweeper" for close-quarter encounters.

Born into a military family in 1860, John T. Thompson quickly distinguished himself as a soldier and, during the Spanish-American War in 1898, became the youngest colonel appointed in the army. He became a munitions expert and even helped form a Gatling gun unit (see *Gatling gun*) that supported then colonel Theodore Roosevelt's bloody charge at San Juan Hill. Three years later, by this time president, Roosevelt requested ordnance tests that would eventually bring Thompson to the Chicago stockyards in 1904 to fire different handguns, calibers, and bullet styles at live cattle (in fairness to the steers, Thompson also used human cadavers to assess various ammunitions). Thompson would have an on-again, off-again relationship with the military forever after.

Thompson retired from the army in 1914 and became a chief engineer for Remington. As World War I was marching along without involvement from U.S. armed forces, Thompson became fascinated by the increased use of trench warfare and convinced that troops could really use a handheld, one-man machine gun that could clear out an enemy's position. Working with the designer of a similar weapon, he began work on a prototype for a charming new compact, large-caliber submachine gun called "the Annihilator." Thompson briefly returned to the military after the United States joined the fight and was a brigadier general in charge of small-arms production before retiring at the war's end in 1918.

Though the Annihilator arrived too late to be used by the military, postwar marketing meetings led its manufacturers to rename it the "Thompson submachine gun" for civilian sales. Costing nearly half the price of a new car, the Thompson soon experienced illicit distribution into the Prohibition-era underworld, where it acquired its street names of "tommy gun," "Chicago typewriter," and "chopper." Gangsters loved it, and it achieved peak notoriety in 1929 following the St. Valentine's Day Massacre, in which Al Capone's henchmen delivered seventy machine-gun bullets and two shotgun blasts into seven of "Bugs" Moran's gang.

It was not until after Thompson's death, at the age of seventy-nine, in 1940 that the U.S. military bought substantial numbers of the weapon for eventual use in World War II, the Korean War, and even Vietnam. Thompson was buried at the U.S. Military Academy at West Point.

Though his namesake was eventually embraced by gangsters and generals alike, its earliest proponent was an unlikely customer—the U.S. Postal Service—which purchased the first tommy guns in 1921 following a rash of mail robberies. Decades later, the now infamous "going postal" madness of the early 1990s led to the eventual prohibition of firearms in all mail facilities.

❖ Maginot ❖

n. a line of fortifications along the frontier of France from Switzerland to Luxembourg, begun in the 1920s as a defense against German invasion and widely considered impregnable, but outflanked in 1940

n. in extended use, indicating a preoccupation with defense (of the status quo, etc.), or with a particular means of defense

—Oxford English Dictionary

Though French foreign minister André Maginot did not live to witness its naming or its inability to withstand the German invasion in World War II, he will forever be associated with one of the greatest military failures in history—the Maginot line.

Born in Paris in 1877, Maginot advanced through the political landscape to become the French undersecretary of war in 1913. Had it not been for the outbreak of World War I, Maginot might likely have led a quiet bureaucratic life, drinking wine and eating cheese. As it was, Maginot quickly enlisted, distinguished himself in combat, and was promoted to sergeant. He was badly wounded in the leg during the defense of Verdun and received France's highest military honor for his bravery—the *médaille militaire*—but his experience of a German invasion stayed with him for life.

The French truly took a glove to the face in World War I, and after the war, there were fewer young Frenchmen, fewer French babies, and a national sense of dread that a future war might be devastating. So France decided to start nesting. After becoming the minister of war in 1922, Maginot began supporting a plan to build a fortified wall, almost two hundred miles long, along France's eastern border from Switzerland to Belgium. He successfully argued that it was a better investment to focus on static defense than modern armor and aircraft. It took four more years to secure funding, but construction finally began in 1930. Sadly, Maginot fell ill after an unsuccessful skirmish with tainted oysters and died of typhoid fever in January 1932 (see also *Typhoid Mary*). Even though he had not conceived of the idea and was not responsible for its actual design (see also *guillotine*), the French decided to name the fortification after their fallen hero.

The Maginot Line was actually a series of self-sufficient forts dug deep into the ground, interspersed with machine-gun posts, tank obstacles, and "pill-box" bunkers. The line was never truly intended as an impregnable defense, only to provide advance warning against a surprise attack. Unfortunately, its construction in the 1930s fostered a false sense of security, and in 1940, German tanks entered France relatively easily by circumventing the line to the north and entering through the Belgian forests. To be fair to the hapless French, the Germans did use high-tech gliders and explosives to break through the Belgian line, and the French forts on the line proper *did* hold. But the subsequent German roughshod run over the French countryside and the fall of Paris within a month led to a lamentable legacy for Maginot and his beloved line.

France constructed a monument to Maginot near Verdun in 1966. Several structures along the Maginot Line were auctioned off to the public in 1969, but the rest lie in decay to this day.

quisling

n. a person cooperating with an occupying enemy force; a collaborator; a traitor

—*Oxford English Dictionary*

Arab diamond traders used to grade gems as first water, second water, and third water—diamonds of the first water being perfect, flawless ones—with water signifying the transparency of the diamonds. Europeans used the Arab grading system for more than three centuries, and the expression *of the first water* has remained in English as a synonym for superlative perfection. Vidkun Quisling was a jackass of the first water, and his last name has been used as a synonym for *traitor* ever since the betrayal of his native country of Norway to the Nazis in World War II.

Quisling was born in the Telemark county of Norway in 1887. He quickly distinguished himself as an extraordinary student and smart aleck by sending in corrections to Norway's national textbook for mathematics while still a young teenager. He became a major in the Norwegian army in his early twenties before moving into politics. In 1933, Quisling and a lawyer friend founded the National Unity Party (*Nasjonal Samling*)—an antidemocratic and anti-Semitic, pro-Fascist and pro-Nazi political group. Quisling, the self-appointed *Fører*—the Norwegian equivalent of Hitler's *Führer*—was only able to muster a small following for his party, and membership was around two thousand on the eve of Germany's invasion of Norway in 1940.

Unfortunately, while most Norwegians considered him to be a bit of a right-wing lunatic, the Nazis had colluded with Quisling in advance of their April 9 attack and planned to capture the king and prime minister and appoint Quisling as the new puppet prime minister. Quisling could not contain himself (or wait for the Nazis) and commandeered a radio station, proclaiming himself the prime minister and insisting that Norwegians cease all resistance to Hitler. Though this initial self-aggrandizement backfired after Quisling received no popular support from his own countrymen, the Nazis did eventually succeed in abolishing the monarchy and appointed Quisling the "minister president" in 1942. Then he really went bonkers.

Quisling began driving around in a bulletproof limousine that was a gift from Hitler. He employed 150 bodyguards and insisted on having official tasters ensure that his food was not poisoned. He issued postage stamps bearing his likeness and insisted that portraits of him be hung all over his palace. Most tragically, he encouraged Norwegians to serve in the Nazi SS, he deported Jews, and he orchestrated the execution of Norwegian patriots.

Once the war ended, the oft-named "Hitler of Norway" was finally arrested on May 9, 1945. The country's civilian courts had not executed anyone in nearly sixty years, but such was the public and political outrage at Quisling that Norway applied its military penal code to allow for the death penalty in anticipation of his case. He was found guilty of treason, murder, and theft, and then executed by firing squad on October 24, 1945.

Quisling's name was used to signify traitorous behavior almost immediately after the 1940 Nazi invasion. Within six days (on April 15), the British newspaper the *Times* had set the brand:

Comment in the Press urges that there should be unremitting vigilance also against possible "Quislings" inside the country.

Using *quisling* to describe a traitor has been common in the press and popular media ever since. For humorous effect, everyone from a cartoon turkey (about Daffy Duck) to *Peanuts'* Linus (about Snoopy) to David Letterman (about *Saturday Night Live*'s Norm MacDonald) have called others quislings.

What is curious is the incredible staying power of Quisling's name. There were certainly other Nazi collaborators whose names were initially used to imply treason—the names of Frenchmen Philippe Pétain and Pierre Laval, in particular, had short-lived infamy—much as Americans still use Benedict Arnold's name today. But it is only Vidkun Quisling whose name was lowercased and dropped into common usage. Perhaps its persistence owes the most to the very satisfying quality it provides as it rolls off the tongue, as the *Times* pointed out in the same April 15, 1940, edition:

To writers, the word *Quisling* is a gift from the gods. If they had been ordered to invent a new word for traitor . . . they could hardly have hit upon a more brilliant combination of letters. Actually it contrives to suggest something at once slippery and tortuous.

❧ Molotov cocktail ❧

n. a makeshift incendiary device for throwing by hand, consisting of a bottle or other breakable container filled with flammable liquid and with a piece of cloth, etc., as a fuse

— *Oxford English Dictionary*

How will history remember perhaps the only man to have shaken hands with Lenin, Stalin, Hitler, Mao Zedong, Churchill, and Franklin Delano Roosevelt? With a riot-rousing, tank-busting, flaming bottle of Finnish pride.

Vyacheslav Mikhailovich Skriabin was born the son of a shop clerk in 1890. Before he turned twenty, he had become a Bolshevik and decided he might bolster his political career by changing his name to Molotov from the Russian word for hammer, *molot*. Though many of his rivals considered him simply a mindless bureaucrat, he eventually became the protégé of Joseph Stalin. He was reviled by some and feared by many. Leon Trotsky famously called him "mediocrity personified," while Winston Churchill considered him "a man of outstanding ability and cold-blooded ruthlessness."

Just three months after Germany invaded Poland in September 1939, sparking World War II, the Soviet Union attacked Finland and began what would be called the Winter War. Struggling against woefully outnumbered but frustratingly plucky Finnish snipers and camouflaged ski troops, the Soviets began relying on the RRAB-3, a cluster-bomb dispenser. As Soviet foreign minister, Molotov insisted in radio broadcasts that Russia was dropping food, not bombs, on Finland— which led the starving Finns to dub the RRAB-3 "Molotov's breadbasket." The Finns had been using incendiary devices developed during the Spanish Civil War three years earlier to combat the invading Soviet tanks and began calling them "Molotov cocktails," as "a drink to go with the food."

Molotov's name came to encompass both the flaming mixture of ethanol, tar, and gasoline and the bottle that delivered it. The devices proved to be so successful that nearly a half million were mass-produced (and bundled with matches) during the Winter War. Early prototypes with burning rags in the mouth of the bottle were replaced by storm matches attached to the bottle and then to ones that ignited on impact.

By the mid-1950s, Nikita Khrushchev and other Communist leaders began denouncing Stalin's legacy, and Molotov was first removed as foreign minister and then expelled from the Communist Party altogether in 1961. He was eventually allowed to rejoin the party in 1984 but died two years later at the age of ninety-six. The Soviet Union dissolved five years later.

Early in his career, the Soviet leader's name was also attached to the Molotov-Ribbentrop Pact between Hitler and Stalin, a nonaggression treaty that lasted only two years before Hitler turned his conquering eyes from France to the Soviet Union. But this association is just a historical footnote. Molotov's etymological infamy will forever reside with his "breadbasket" and, especially, "cocktail" namesakes—somewhat ironically, as Molotov was actually a teetotaling vegetarian.

⟨ ЯК-47 ⟩

n. an automatic kalashnikov rifle; esp. a model of this rifle, first manufactured in 1947

— *Oxford English Dictionary*

Mikhail Kalashnikov, the quiet and conscientious creator of one of the most notorious weapons in history, insists that it is only historical circumstance that led him to create assault rifles instead of lawnmowers.

Atomic weapons and firebombings aside, World War II featured cramped combat between troops that necessitated special equipment. Unlike the British more than one hundred years earlier who wanted to be able to kill more people at a distance (see *shrapnel*), the Germans realized that most rifles were too powerful for close encounters and wanted a weapon that could wreak havoc in tight quarters (see *tommy gun*). Hitler referred to their first mass-deployment creation as a *Sturmgewehr*, "storm rifle," which became translated to "assault rifle." The Russians were assaulted repeatedly by the German wonder gun and were duly impressed.

Mikhail Kalashnikov was a tank driver in the Red

Army in 1938 and got promoted to commander before being wounded by Germans during the Battle of Bryansk in 1941. As he was recovering from his injuries, he began thinking about how best to drive the German hordes from his homeland. As he later mused, "It is the Germans who are responsible for the fact that I became a fabricator of arms. If not for them, I would have constructed agricultural machines." Kalashnikov decided to start entering gun-building contests and finally came up big in 1947. His invention was special because it was a true assault rifle (good for shooting on the run), had selective fire (semiautomatic for judicious firing and fully automatic for a kill-crazy rampage), was gas-powered (cartridges were almost magically chambered and ejected), and, most important, was cheap, durable, and easy to use—even in the cold and muddy conditions of the Russian front.

The Soviet army officially accepted the Avtomat Kalashnikova model 1947 (AK-47) in 1949, and in the six decades since, more AK rifles have been produced than all other assault rifles combined. Kalashnikov was promoted to lieutenant general but claims never to have profited from the more than 100 million weapons bearing his name circulating around the world, surviving instead on a state pension. "My work is my life, and my life is my work. I invented this assault rifle to defend my country. Today, I am proud that it has become synonymous with liberty."

The AK-47 appears on the flags of Mozambique and Hezbollah, the coats of arms of Zimbabwe and East Timor, and the logo of the Iranian Islamic

Revolutionary Guard Corps. Kalashnikov himself is philosophical about his namesake and is apparently impervious to insomnia. "If someone asks me how I can sleep at night knowing that my arms have killed millions of people, I respond that I have no problem sleeping, my conscience is clean."

There are a museum and a monument honoring the gun designer in Izhevsk, Russia, where he still lives, but it is perhaps Samuel L. Jackson's character in Quentin Tarantino's film *Jackie Brown* who sums up Kalashnikov's legacy most eloquently. "AK-47 . . . When you absolutely, positively got to kill every motherfucker in the room, accept no substitutes."

⊰ Big Bertha ⊱

n. any very large cannon

—*Webster's New Universal Unabridged Dictionary,*

Second Edition

After Bertha Krupp's father died in 1902, she became the sole inheritor of the most powerful armament and munitions empire in Germany, provided the moniker for some freakishly large artillery, and eventually saw her name attached to a munitions factory that employed and abused concentration camp inmates.

Bertha Krupp was born in Essen, Germany, in 1886—home of her family's steelworks since 1811. Her father, Friedrich "Fritz" Alfred Krupp, had successfully expanded the company into a world-class arms manufacturer and was creating cannons that used Alfred Nobel's improved gunpowder (see *Nobel Prize*) by the turn of the twentieth century. Unfortunately, Fritz also seemed to have a penchant for young boys and was caught in a sordid scandal of alleged pederasty that landed his beleaguered wife in an insane asylum and caused his death (reportedly by stroke, but most believe by suicide) in 1902. The kaiser, Wilhelm II, decided that sixteen-year-old heiress Bertha could not possibly take over one of Germany's most important manufacturers, so he forced her to marry diplomat Gustav von Bohlen und Halbach, who assumed the name Krupp and administrative control of the company.

Frau Bertha Krupp von Bohlen und Halbach proved to be more formidable than the kaiser (or her husband) anticipated, and she was instrumental in helping Gustav run the company. In 1914, the Krupp factory produced an extraordinary 420-millimeter, short-barreled and high-trajectory (howitzer) monstrosity. Its designers called it *Dicke Bertha* (Fat Bertha) in honor of the Krupp heiress and owner, and it wreaked havoc on French and Belgian forts during the early part of World War I. The original Fat Bertha paved the way for even larger and longer-ranged howitzers that were all generally dubbed "Big Berthas" by the Allied troops that suffered under their shells. The Paris Gun was one of the later Bertha types used to bombard the City of Light in 1918. Its shells weighed more than two hundred pounds and traveled so high (twenty-five miles) and so far (more than eighty miles) that gunners had to factor in the rotation of the Earth when making their trajectory calculations.

Incredibly, the heavy howitzers of World War I are not even Bertha Krupp's most notorious namesakes. By 1942, intense aerial attacks led the Third Reich to spread out its artillery production beyond the range of Allied bombers. The Krupp company opened a munitions plant in Markstädt (occupied Poland) and named it after its matriarch—the Berthawerk. Unfortunately, labor was scarce, so the Berthawerk used prisoners from the nearby Fünfteichen concentration camp for its frantic production. Bertha's son Alfried eventually assumed control of the company, was indicted for crimes against humanity (for using and mistreating camp inmates), and was sentenced to twelve years in prison during the postwar Nuremberg trials. His conviction was overturned in 1951 by the U.S. high commissioner in Germany, in part because the United States believed it needed strong German industry to help Europe recover and stave off a new global threat—communism (see *McCarthyism*).

As the mere heiress to the Krupp dynasty, Bertha was never accused of any wrongdoing. She was reunited with Alfried in 1951 and moved with him back to Essen, where she lived until her death in 1957.

· CHAPTER FOUR·

Lust & Lies

⊲❴Messalina❵⊳

n. a licentious, lascivious, or scheming woman
— *Oxford English Dictionary*

Valeria Messalina managed to establish an extraordinarily nasty reputation for herself as a manipulative and cuckolding floozy, all before even turning thirty. Once the most powerful woman in the Roman Empire, she was eventually beheaded and remembered in her own time and by posterity as one of history's vilest women.

The date and location of Messalina's birth are unknown, but it was most likely in Rome circa AD 20, and it was to a royal line. Her great-granduncle Augustus had been Rome's first emperor. While still a teenager, she became the third wife of Claudius, who was himself the aging uncle of the sexually deviant current emperor, Caligula. After Caligula's assassination and

Claudius's succession to the throne, the new empress, Messalina, became a nymphomaniacal tyrant.

Messalina's sexploits are legendary, with the most famous being her twenty-four-hour sausage contest with a local prostitute to see who could endure the most part-ners. According to Pliny's account in *Naturalis Historia*, Messalina was the grand victor with an aching total of twenty-five. Other historians purport that she not only owned and operated a brothel but also served as one of its most enthusiastic employees, under an assumed name. Despite her young age, Messalina was also a shrewd and calculating political operator. She bore two children with Claudius and knew that her son was next in line to be emperor. Seeking to maximize her assets, she allegedly slept with wealthy landowners, had them tried and con-victed of false treason, and then assumed control of their properties. She further convinced poor Claudius to exile and execute anyone whom she found threatening.

In a fit of sex-fueled delusion during one of Claudius's many business trips, Messalina ultimately sealed her own doom. She forced one of her lovers (the strapping and flamboyantly named Gaius Silius) to divorce his wife, marry her in a bigamous public ceremony, plot the assassination of Claudius, and attempt to assume the throne. Unfortunately for them, Claudius was alerted to their treachery and quickly ordered that both should be dispatched. After the fact, Claudius seemed relatively nonplussed by the scandal and reportedly ordered more wine after being informed of their eventual executions. In the years that followed, despite the Senate's order to remove the statues and other signs of her across the empire, her name quickly emerged and endured to represent any deceitful and unfaithful woman.

Beyond her unflattering eponym, Messalina's name has since been invoked by authors ranging from Charlotte Brontë to Toni Morrison to Gabriel García Márquez, while her sexual exploits have specifically served as fictional fodder for Mario Puzo, Chuck Palahniuk, and even Leopold von Sacher-Masoch (see *masochism*). But it was early Roman author Juvenal who offered the most stinging recap of her legacy. Though Juvenal is notorious in his own right as an unapologetic misogynist, he seemed to capture the sentiment of the times when he described her (in a translation by Peter Green) as a "whore-empress . . . exhausted by men, yet a long way from satisfied, cheeks grimed with lamp-smoke, filthy, carrying home to her Imperial couch the stink of the whorehouse."

◅ Casanova ▻

n. a man who is a promiscuous and unscrupulous lover
—*Merriam-Webster's Collegiate Dictionary, Eleventh Edition*

Some would surely argue that an accepted record of seducing scores of partners should be a sterling achievement, but it seems rather a shallow legacy for an extraordinary man with extraordinary talents. Though nowhere near basketball legend Wilt Chamberlain's purported bedding of twenty thousand women, the man known today simply as Casanova still put up some eyebrow-raising numbers. Casanova's spectacular exploits may have been lost to history were it not for *Histoire de ma vie* (*Story of My Life*)—his 1.5-million-word, twelve-volume memoir chronicling his 120-plus sexual conquests (both female and male)—and his extraordinary travels across eighteenth-century Europe. As a result, Casanova will forever be remembered as a great lover, but this is mere overshadowing of the fact that he was also a great intellectual, businessman, and con artist.

Giacomo Casanova de Seingalt was born in Venice in 1725 to an actress and any one of several possible men. He was a sensitive child, prone to nosebleeds, who was raised primarily in the care of a priest and his family. He had his first sexual experience at the age of eleven, earned a law degree by the age of seventeen, and began and abandoned careers as a priest, soldier, gambler, and violinist all by the age of twenty-one.

By the age of thirty, he had lived in Venice and then Paris, was imprisoned and had escaped. He became a prominent alchemist and spy, and sold tickets for France's first state lottery and then French bonds to support the Seven Years' War (see *silhouette* and *sadism*). He made a fortune and quickly lost it maintaining his extravagant and promiscuous lifestyle. He attempted to restore his wealth in England by proposing a state lottery system there but succeeded in acquiring nothing but venereal disease and an understanding that the English "have a special character . . . which makes them think they are superior to everyone else. It is a belief shared by all nations, each thinking itself the best. And they are all right."

Casanova likewise failed to convince Frederick the Great in Germany and Catherine the Great in Russia (see *Potemkin*) that state lotteries were their ticket to greater prosperity. He continued his travels and conquests while publishing plays, essays, and a three-volume translation of the *Iliad*; contemplating balloon travel with Benjamin Franklin; and debating theology with Voltaire, but his health began to wane and he took up a position as a librarian. Unaccustomed to a sedentary lifestyle, he briefly considered suicide but opted instead to pen his life story, which unapologetically reveled in its introduction, "I have delighted in going astray and I have constantly lived in error, with no other consolation than that of knowing I have erred."

He died in 1798 at the age of seventy-three, and his last words would seem at odds with his cultural legacy as a sexual conquistador: "I have lived as a philosopher and I die as a Christian."

⋖[sadism]⋗

n. the getting of sexual pleasure from dominating, mistreating, or hurting one's partner, physically or otherwise

—*Webster's New Universal Unabridged Dictionary,*
Second Edition

As is the case with the term for *wanting* to be domi-
nated (see *masochism*), this psychological condition was
also coined by psychiatrist Richard von Krafft-Ebing
in 1886, who, once again, chose a literary source for
his inspiration—the Marquis de Sade, a revolutionary
French novelist whose dogged attainment of personal
pleasure resulted in his spending nearly half of his life
in prisons and insane asylums.

Donatien Alphonse François, the Marquis de Sade,
was born into Paris high society in 1740. Before writing the novels that would explore the libertine pursuits of bestiality, necrophilia, and juvenile rape, the
young Sade had an aristocratic upbringing, alternating
between the titles *comte* (count) and *marquis* (marquess)
and rising to the rank of colonel during the sweeping
Seven Years' War. Despite marriage and the arrival of
three children, Sade gained notoriety in Paris for his
frequent employment and (especially) abuse of young
prostitutes, resulting in his nearly constant surveil-
lance by the police.

After being imprisoned several times, accused of the
then serious crime of blasphemy, and widely rumored
to be having an affair with his wife's sister, Sade was
exiled to his château at Lacoste in Provence in 1768,
the year after his father's death. Deeper scandal ensued
later that year when a young woman (perhaps a prostitute) claimed she was imprisoned and sexually abused
by him before escaping through a second-story window. Four years later, he and a male servant were forced
to flee to Italy (with his wife's sister) after in absentia

convictions and death sentences for sodomy and the near-fatal poisoning of several prostitutes with a supposed aphrodisiac. More upset by his extramarital affair than by his more colorful exploits, his mother-in-law obtained a royal order of arrest and imprisonment.

After five years of secretive return trips to Lacoste, punctuated by repeated accusations of sexual mistreatment by young employees (the father of one nearly succeeded in shooting the marquis at point-blank range), Sade was eventually arrested and imprisoned. He successfully appealed his death sentence but still spent eleven years behind bars and was transferred from the Bastille to an insane asylum a mere ten days before the storming of the famed prison on July 14, 1789— the start of the French Revolution. He was ultimately released a year later, and his wife divorced him soon after.

Sade wrote most of his most controversial fiction while in the Bastille, including *The 120 Days of Sodom*, which catalogs the horrific exploits of four aristocrats who seal themselves in a castle for four months with four prostitutes and forty-six teenagers whom they sexually abuse and torture before slaughtering them. Likewise, *Justine* and *Juliette* chronicle the experiences of two sisters. Justine is the virtuous one, forced to become a sex slave in a monastery and eventually struck by lightning. Juliette, in contrast, is a nymphomaniac who enjoys an orgy with the pope and dies happy.

As with Leopold von Sacher-Masoch and masochism, the Austrian psychiatrist Richard von Krafft-Ebing

felt that Sade and his writings represented the embodi-
ment of the sexual pathology that enjoys gratification
from domination and abuse. Nearly seventy-five years
after the Marquis de Sade's death, Krafft-Ebing coined
the term *sadism* in his landmark *Psychopathia Sexualis*
in 1886. Sigmund Freud eventually noted that tenden-
cies toward sadism and masochism are often found in
the same individuals and thus created the term *sado-
masochism* (commonly, *S&M*).

Most of Sade's descendants have vigorously tried to
dissociate themselves from his name, with the exception of the Comte Xavier de Sade, who found a trunk of
letters and manuscripts in 1948 that he allowed to be
published over the next twelve years, renewing interest
in the controversial author in the 1960s.

After his initial release from the asylum, Sade himself
became a political radical during the guillotine-crazed
Reign of Terror following the French Revolution. However, despite publishing both *Justine* and *Juliette* anony-
mously after his release from the Bastille, his identity
was discovered by Napoleon, who had him incarcerated
for the remainder of his life—first in prison and then,
after Sade attempted to seduce young fellow prisoners, again in an insane asylum. Sade began an affair
with the daughter of a worker at the asylum that lasted
four years—until his death in 1814. She was thirteen
years old.

⊰ masochism ⊱

n. the getting of sexual pleasure from being domi-
nated, mistreated, or hurt physically or otherwise
by one's partner

— *Webster's New Universal Unabridged Dictionary,*
Second Edition

Our psychological term for this sexual fetish was coined
by a psychiatrist in 1886 but inspired by author Leopold von Sacher-Masoch, who is destined to be remembered not for his writings on anti-Semitism or women's
suffrage but for his secret penchant for domination by
women wearing fur.

Sacher-Masoch was born in 1836 in a province of the
Austrian Empire that is now part of Ukraine. Raised
in a Roman Catholic household with a police chief as
a father, Sacher-Masoch's early writings as a professor
were fairly standard Austrian fare—history, folklore,
and ethnic short stories. But it was 1870's *Venus in Furs*,
the only one of his short novels still commonly available in English, that brought him notoriety. It was the
first glimpse into his particular fetishes and described
in detail his fantasy of dominant fur-clad women.

Sacher-Masoch found a willing partner with an early
mistress, Baroness Fanny Pistor—herself an emerging
writer who approached him for help with her work.
Sacher-Masoch eventually coaxed Pistor into signing
a contract that enslaved him to her for a period of six
months in 1869, with his only stipulation being that

she should wear furs as much as possible. Their experiences served as the fodder for *Venus in Furs*, in which the main character asks to be degraded by his dominatrix and is eventually further abused by a trio of African women. Unfortunately, he found less willingness to indulge his fantasies from his first wife, Aurora von Römelin, whom he married in 1873 and eventually divorced over obvious "irreconcilable differences." He eventually married his assistant.

It was around Sacher-Masoch's fiftieth birthday that psychiatrist Richard von Krafft-Ebing introduced the term *masochism* in his famous series of case studies of sexual perversity, *Psychopathia Sexualis*. The Latin title was a deliberate attempt to discourage reading by an enthusiastic lay audience with purely prurient interests in such formerly taboo topics as female sexual pleasure and "contrary sexual desires." Krafft-Ebing was a strict procreationist and believed that any sexual activity strictly for gratification was perverse (interestingly, while rape was considered deviant, it was not strictly perverse in that pregnancy could still result).

To the great dismay of Sacher-Masoch, Krafft-Ebing co-opted the author's name to describe gratification derived from receiving pain or humiliation: "I feel justified in calling this sexual anomaly 'Masochism,' because the author Sacher-Masoch frequently made this perversion, which up to his time was quite unknown to the scientific world as such, the substratum of his writings. . . . During recent years facts have been advanced which prove that Sacher-Masoch was not only the poet of Masochism, but that he himself was afflicted with the anomaly." In fact, the specific details of Sacher-Masoch's private life were relatively unknown until his first wife's memoirs were published in 1905.

Sigmund Freud, a contemporary of Krafft-Ebing, would eventually assert that the impulse for masochism is often accompanied by an impulse for sadism (gratification derived from *inflicting* pain or humiliation)— a term based on the life and writings of the Marquis de Sade (see *sadism*).

Despite founding an association for adult education with his second wife in 1893 and becoming a tireless opponent of anti-Semitism and an equally tireless supporter of women's rights late in his life, Sacher-Masoch's name is inextricably linked with sexual deviance— beyond the clinical diagnosis, he and *Venus in Furs* have been pop-referenced by bands ranging from the Velvet Underground to Marilyn Manson to Bauhaus.

Masoch spent the last years of his life under psychiatric care in Germany. He died in 1895.

⊲ Mata Hari ⊳

n. a woman likened in some way to Mata Hari; esp. a beautiful and seductive female spy

—*Oxford English Dictionary*

These two words are the pop culture relic of one woman's infamous journey from Dutch kindergarten teacher to Parisian exotic dancer to German sex spy to firing-squad target.

Though most frequently associated with Parisian nightlife and international espionage, Mata Hari was actually born in the Netherlands in 1876 with a decidedly unsexy name—Margaretha Geertruida Zelle. Her father was a successful investor and hat-store owner, and young Margaretha enjoyed a fairly swank life until her early teens, when things got a little rough. In short order, her mother died, her father remarried, she moved in with her godfather, and she had to abandon her studies to be a kindergarten teacher after attracting the lustful eye of her headmaster. By eighteen, she was primed and ready for an unhealthy marriage.

In 1895 Margaretha answered a lonely hearts ad in a Dutch newspaper and wed an abusive and alcoholic army officer named Rudolf John MacLeod. The unlikely pair moved to Java in the Dutch East Indies and had two children and at least one extramarital affair apiece. The philanderers divorced before too long, and Margaretha moved to Paris to become a circus performer named Lady MacLeod. Within two years, she assumed the stage name of Mata Hari, "Eye of the Dawn" in Malay, and pretended to be a Java princess. Few questioned her pedigree, bewitched as they were by the fact that her act of provocative Indonesian dances ended with her wearing little more than a jeweled brassiere. She was a nearly overnight sensation and soon had ample work as a dancer and courtesan. Her free spirit and revealing wardrobe made her the toast of a generous company of financiers, politicians, and military men, and she traveled extensively across the continent.

When World War I broke out, Mata Hari was still able to travel around freely, as she was still a citizen of the neutral Netherlands. This, in addition to her relations with high-ranking officials, drew the attention of military intelligence on both sides of the English Channel. When interrogated by the British, she claimed to be a French agent. However, the French later intercepted a coded message identifying a German spy known only as H-21 whom they deduced to be Mata Hari.

Though one prosecutor later admitted that "there wasn't enough evidence to flog a cat," Mata Hari was arrested and found guilty of spying and causing the deaths of nearly fifty thousand soldiers. She was executed by firing squad on October 15, 1917. Rumors surrounding the theatrics of her death abound. Some claim that she opened her coat to flash her executioners and blew them a kiss, while all seem to agree that she demurely declined her blindfold.

Greta Garbo cemented the fantasy of her role as seductive sex spy in 1931's *Mata Hari*. Only in 2017, when the French army releases classified documents about her trial and execution, will we have a clearer understanding of the true story behind this archetypal femme fatale.

❧ Mae West ❧

n. an inflatable life jacket, originally one issued to
R.A.F. servicemen in the Second World War

— *Oxford English Dictionary*

Mae West once coyly asked a police escort, "Is that a
pistol in your pocket, or are you happy to see me?" Her
buxom figure and unapologetic bawdiness made her a
box office star and a favorite of World War II British
flyboys, who notoriously named their life jackets after
her, alleging that they "bulged in all the right places."

Given her extraordinary career as a sex symbol that
extended (perhaps regrettably) all the way into the
1970s, it may be difficult to believe that Mae West was
born way back in 1893 in Brooklyn. Then Mary Jane
West, she was the daughter of a prizefighter and corset
model and was a professional vaudevillian by the time
she was fourteen. Her "Baby Mae" character segued into
male impersonation, blackface, and suggestive and sala-
cious shimmying. Her big breakthrough came when she
wrote, produced, directed, and starred in her first Broad-
way play in 1926—titled, simply, *Sex*. It was hugely
popular, but the entire crew was eventually arrested for
obscenity, and West even spent a few days in prison—"in
her silk underpants," she later confessed—before being
released for good behavior. Subsequent plays brought on
fussbudgety objections from the New York Society for
the Suppression of Vice (see *Comstockery*) and more police
attention, but by that point, West was a star.

West was already thirty-eight years old when Hollywood came knocking in 1932, and she stunned everyone by successfully rewriting her roles to carve out a full-figured niche for herself. In her film debut, she famously responded to a young girl's breathless comment, "Goodness! What lovely diamonds!" by saying, "Goodness had nothing to do with it, dearie" (which would eventually become the title of her bestselling autobiography). Audiences adored her, and the conservative Production Code officers loathed her. She made nine more films in the thirties and early forties before switching to radio and getting herself banned from NBC radio after her "Eve" character told Don Ameche's "Adam" that "I feel like doin' a big apple."

West maintained her sex-bomb persona into her twilight years, turning down the starring role in 1950's *Sunset Boulevard* at nearly sixty because she was convinced she was as sexy as ever and would not be convincing as a has-been actress. She recorded three rock-and-roll albums in the late 1960s, including the double-entendred *Great Balls of Fire* in 1968 (at seventy-five); and in 1976 (at eighty-four) she starred in her last film, *Sextette*, in which she played an aging sex symbol that everyone wants to bed, including her former husbands (played by George Hamilton, Ringo Starr, and Tony Curtis) and an entire unidentifiable U.S. "athletic" team.

West died at home in 1980 at the age of eighty-seven, and her name is still used to this day in reference to certain military life jackets as well as a bulging, two-lobed, unfortunately malfunctioning parachute. Most modern actresses would likely eschew having their torso compared to an inflatable rubber vest or bulky parachute, but West once advised women to "cultivate your curves—they may be dangerous, but they won't be avoided."

⊲ in like Flynn ⊳

n. to be immediately or emphatically successful, often in a sexual or romantic context

—*Oxford English Dictionary*

The origin of this phrase occasionally points to Edward J. Flynn, who was an extraordinarily successful campaign manager for New York's Democratic Party during the Franklin Delano Roosevelt era. But the far more notorious and most widely accepted theory is that it appeared after swaggering actor Errol Flynn successfully evaded conviction on two charges of statutory rape in the early 1940s.

Despite his numerous appearances in British costume dramas and American westerns, Errol Leslie Flynn was actually born in Tasmania in 1909. His exploits started early on, with expulsions from grammar schools in Sydney for fighting and, apparently, rolling in the sheets with a school laundress. In his twenties, he was an utter failure as a tobacco farmer and copper miner in Papua New Guinea, so he turned to acting and moved first to England and then to the United States, where he would become an international film icon.

Flynn starred in more than fifty films in a career that spanned from the early 1930s to the late 1950s. Among many other roles, he often appeared as a swashbuckler, gunslinger, or soldier (despite being rejected by each of the armed services for a bad heart, tuberculosis, and malaria). By all accounts, he was also an unapologetic and charming womanizer, whose on-screen charisma was matched only by his off-screen conquests. He was always married but never faithful, reportedly bedding starlets by the dozen. Amid recurring bouts with the abuse of alcohol, heroin, and his marital vows, he had three wives and four children.

In 1942 his bohemian lifestyle took a dark turn when he was accused of raping not one but two under-age girls. Flynn claimed that Hollywood was trying to make him a scapegoat for the excesses of the studio system. His friends and associates formed the American Boys' Club for the Defense of Errol Flynn (ABCDEF), and he was eventually cleared of all charges by an all-female jury. Ironically (or appropriately), Flynn had previously played the Earl of Essex, himself famous for pardoning a convicted rapist (see *derrick*), in 1939's *Private Lives of Elizabeth and Essex*. Rather than ruining his reputation, the scandal seemed only to burnish his persona as the consummate ladies' man, and the phrase *in like Flynn* entered the lexicon as a winking badge of honor.

For most of the 1950s, Flynn lived with his third wife in Jamaica but still made several movies in spite of his aging appearance and failing health. He had one final affair, with a fifteen-year-old actress, and allegedly planned to marry her before dying of a massive heart attack in 1959. However, Flynn could not remain far from scandal for long, even in death. After the posthumous publication of his autobiography—*My Wicked, Wicked Ways*—unauthorized biographies began popping up with largely unsubstantiated allegations that he had been a Nazi spy and a bisexual lover of Howard Hughes and Truman Capote.

As for his cultural legacy, Flynn always seemed proud of his infamous catchphrase. He never quite liked the title of his autobiography but was unsuccessful in lobbying his publisher to consider another—*In Like Me*.

❧ Barbie ❧

> *n.* a woman who is likened to a Barbie doll, esp. in being pretty or shapely but passive, characterless, or unintelligent
>
> —*Oxford English Dictionary*

The original "Barbie" was a preteen girl whose mother was convinced she would like to play with a German fashion doll for men, while the original "Ken" was her hapless brother who had the misfortune of being the only boy around when names were bandied about for

Barbie's on-again, off-again, sexually unthreatening "play pal."

It all started with a sexy German toy sold in European bars and tobacco shops in the 1950s. Ruth and Elliot Handler bought several while traveling in Switzerland in 1956 and thought their daughter, Barbara, would prefer them to the standard American doll fare of the day. Under Ruth's guidance, Elliot's burgeoning toy company, Mattel, tweaked the design, named the plastic figure after their daughter, and introduced "Barbie" at the New York City toy fair in 1959. Two years later, in a marketing move that might just be as creepy as it sounds, the Handlers named Barbie's boyfriend "Ken" after their real-life son, Kenneth.

Ruth wanted her daughter and all young girls to have a doll that looked like a woman, and full breasts were always an essential part of the design. The original prototypes from the Japanese manufacturer were apparently so realistic that Mattel executives had to file down the nipples to make them less provocative, but the original proportions were still outrageous. The first Barbies on the market (a staggering 350,000 were sold in the first year alone), if extrapolated to human scale, would have had the unstable female measurements of a thirty-nine-inch chest, an eighteen-inch waist, and thirty-three-inch hips.

Social critics plagued Barbie from the beginning, and the new dolls sauntering on the scene often did not help matters. Slumber Party Barbie, issued in 1965, came with a bathroom scale indicating she weighed 110 pounds (approximately 35 pounds underweight, given her projected five-foot-nine-inch height), and her packaging included a book on weight loss that advised girls not to eat. Researchers in Finland later theorized that a life-size Barbie would lack the body fat necessary to menstruate. Subsequent releases of Barbie warned girls that "Math class is tough!" and rolled around in wheelchairs that could not fit in the elevator of her own Dream House.

And yet still they sold and continue to sell—two every second (if Mattel executives are to be believed)—in more than 150 countries. The word *Barbie* took on its derogatory bimbo meaning in the early 1970s, and the artistic backlash against the doll over the last thirty-five years has included putting Barbie bits into blenders; dressing Barbies in S&M outfits (see *sadism* and *masochism*); and creating countless parodies in print, television, and plastic. Daughter Barbara Handler seemed always to resent the association to her plastic namesake. "Much of me is very proud that my folks invented the doll. I just wish I wasn't attached to it."

The epilogue of Barbie's inventor is a remarkable story in and of itself, as the shape of women's breasts once again provided the inspiration for her last commercial venture. Ruth Handler was diagnosed with breast cancer in 1970. Following a mastectomy, she ended up manufacturing a new, more realistic prosthetic for women—the "Nearly Me." Doctor Barbie—who debuted in 1987 with the tagline "She changes from doctor to glorious date!"—could not have been prouder.

CHAPTER FIVE

Science & Philosophy

⊰ mithridate ⊱

n. any of various medicinal preparations, usually in the form of an electuary compounded of many ingredients, believed to be a universal antidote to poison or a panacea

⊰ mithridatize ⊱

v. to render immune to or tolerant of a poison, esp. by the administration of gradually increasing doses
—*Oxford English Dictionary*

Shakespeare's oft-misquoted Henry IV once opined that "Uneasy lies the head that wears a crown," which was never more true than for Mithridates VI. Though notoriously successful through countless acts of homicide, matricide, genocide, and even dual sororicide/mariticide, Mithridates was an abject failure in one important killing—his own suicide.

Thirteen centuries before Osman I (see *ottoman*) became the sultan of Anatolia in what is modern-day Turkey, teenage Mithridates became the king of Pontus in northern Anatolia around 120 BC. In short order, he threw his mother in prison and married his sister (both of whom he would eventually murder) to protect his power. After invading western Anatolia, he ordered the apocalyptic execution of eighty thousand Roman civilians, kicking off the First and Second Mithridatic Wars and the eventual assassinations of his two sons, each of whom tried to overthrow him.

Mithridates was so paranoid near the end of his life that he allegedly slept with farm animals in his room to alert him of intruders and killed all of his concubines so that his precious harem might not fall prey to Roman invaders. After finally being conquered by Pompey, Mithridates tried unsuccessfully to poison himself rather than suffer capture. Unfortunately, out of social-phobic delusions, Mithridates had spent years carefully accustoming himself to small doses of poison to avert potential treachery and apparently succeeded in making himself immune. In abject despair, he was forced, in 63 BC, to order a servant to kill him with a sword.

When Pompey ransacked Mithridates' home, he allegedly discovered the king's formula for a single complex antidote to all known poisons. He delivered it to Rome, where it was translated and revised over time under various names, including mithridatium, theriac, and Venice treacle, and prescribed throughout the Middle Ages and the Renaissance and even into the nineteenth century. Made of a hodgepodge of opium, turpentine, pepper, and dozens of other ingredients (including viper flesh), the concoction was used to treat poisonous bites, general illnesses, and even the plague. It had its skeptics, however, with Pliny famously mocking, "The Mithridatic antidote is composed of fifty-four ingredients, no two of them having the same weight. . . . Which of the gods . . . fixed these absurd proportions? It is plainly a showy parade of the art, and a colossal boast of science."

As for Mithridates' self-immunization, the act of mithridatizing is primarily practiced today only by zoo handlers and venom researchers. However, the concept has been used in fiction by Dumas' Count of Monte Cristo and Hawthorne's daughter of Rappaccini as well as to hilarious effect in the book and film *The Princess Bride*, when the hero wins a "battle of wits" "to the death" by surviving a poisonous ingestion of fictional "iocane powder" after having built up a resistance to it.

"Inconceivable!"

❧ gibberish ❧

n. rapid and inarticulate talk; unintelligible chatter;
jargon

—*Webster's New Universal Unabridged Dictionary,*
Second Edition

Insofar as etymologists fight, scuffle, and quibble in
their dusty cubicles, the origin of *gibberish* is somewhat hotly contested. The most popular theory,
however, is that it derives from eighth-century alchemist Jabir ibn Hazyan, whose name was latinized to
Geber and who penned his formulas in anagrams and
obtuse jargon to (as he once wrote) "baffle and lead
into error everyone except those whom God loves and
provides for."

Despite his prolific authorship (more than two thousand books were allegedly written by him), much of
Geber's heritage, life, and legacy remain shrouded in
mystery. He is believed to have been born in the early
eighth century and to have died in the early ninth. He
might have been Arabian or Persian, was perhaps born
in present-day Iran, and perhaps died in present-day
Iraq. Some researchers maintain that he never existed
at all and was simply a pseudonym for a group of writers attempting to maintain secret identities. However,
there are many who refer to him (instead of Antoine
Lavoisier) as the "father of chemistry," and he is indisputably one of the first to pursue the ever elusive
goals of turning base metals into gold (alchemy) and

discovering the mythical element that might make transmutation possible (the philosopher's stone).

Though his initial scientific goals were somewhat inauspicious (no one ever quite pulled off the alchemical miracle), Geber is believed to have developed dozens of pieces of laboratory equipment still in use today (including early alembics for distillation), discovered a baker's dozen of elements and acids (including sulfur and mercury), and improved a score of manufacturing processes (including steelmaking and leather tanning). But it is his encrypted writings on alchemy that still mystify readers today. Unfortunately, in one of its very few short shrifts, the venerable *Oxford English Dictionary* seems hesitant to give Geber his potential due, positing that *gibberish* derives from *gibber*, despite the latter not appearing until 1604, fifty years after the former (1554). Followers of this theory put *gibberish* into the nonsense cabinet of onomatopoeic words such as *gabble* and *jabber*, though many concede its use may have been influenced by Geber's name.

Whatever its origins, gibberish has been a staple of literature, science, entertainment, and even politics ever since. "O frabjous day! Callooh! Callay!" from Lewis Carroll's "Jabberwocky" provides many children with their first introduction to nonsense speech, while the Japanese term *mojibake* (character change) is the name for the garbled and unreadable text that appears on your computer from improperly coded characters. Scat singers since the turn of the twentieth century have conjured up improvisational jazz vocals, while *The Muppet Show*'s Swedish Chef punctuated his culinary gibberish with the exclamatory "Börk! Börk! Börk!" Finally, James Joyce has confounded countless readers of 1939's Finnegan's Wake with a host of idiosyncratic, multilingual, and portmanteau words (see also *gerrymander*), while real-life U.S. Representative Maury Maverick coined the term *gobbledygook* in 1944 to describe what he condemned as the "convoluted language of bureaucrats."

Sometimes, however, gibberish is simply in the eye of the beholder. In *The Lost Symbol*—bestselling wordsmith Dan Brown's sequel to *The Da Vinci Code*—jet-setting Harvard symbologist Robert Langdon condescendingly educates mere mind-body scientist Dr. Katherine Solomon on the tricks of his trade and raises the literary veil on what it is difficult to believe she finds unintelligible.

> "Actually, Katherine, it's not gibberish." His eyes brightened again with the thrill of discovery. "It's . . . Latin."

◄❧ dunce ❧►

n. a dull, ignorant person
— *Webster's New Universal Unabridged Dictionary,*
Second Edition

Two great tragedies befell the brilliant scholar and subtle philosopher John Duns Scotus. The first is that he had the misfortune to drop into a coma in fourteenth-century Germany—prompting the now-defunct but then-obligatory live burial. The second is that a few of his dim-witted followers ruined his legacy by shunning the enlightenment of the Renaissance in his name, earning eternal dunce caps for all.

No one knows for certain when or where theologian John Duns Scotus was born, though it is believed to have been near the end of the thirteenth century and, based on his middle name, either in Duns (Scotland), Dunse (Berwickshire), or Dunston (Northumberland). What is known is that he proved to be an intellectual wonder first at Oxford and then at the University of Paris, where he lectured in 1302. He was an ordained Franciscan priest and is perhaps the greatest historical defender of the doctrine of the Immaculate Conception of Mary.

Scotus is believed to have died while in his midforties in 1308. Why he fell into a coma is a mystery, but it was surely the subsequent burial while still alive that ultimately killed him. His writings and teachings lived beyond, however, and his Scotist followers helped sustain his philosophies surrounding the "thisness" of things and the existence of God. He was belovedly remembered as the "Subtle Doctor" for the quiet power and nuanced logic of his arguments, and he was a cornerstone of the religious canon for nearly two hundred years.

Unfortunately for Scotus, a shift began taking place in the late fifteenth century. The arguments that had charmed even his rivals in the past were suddenly viewed as sophist, illogical, and theologically obstructionist during the Renaissance. The Scotists (by then called Dunsmen) were increasingly attacked for their unwillingness to accept new scholarship. They railed hopelessly against intellectual progress and subsequently became known collectively as "dunses." One somewhat infamous dunce was Nicholas de Orbellis, a professor of philosophy and adamant follower of Scotus, whose own name came to be shortened to *dorbel*, which the *Oxford English Dictionary* defined in 1533 as "a scholastical pedant, a dull-witted person, dolt," and which might point to the origin of the phrase *dumb as a doorbell*. The final transformation to *dunce* implied a complete inability to learn, and by 1577 the *OED* identified a dunce as "a dull-witted, stupid person; a dullard, blockhead"—a far cry from the intellectual powerhouse of its namesake (see also *epicure*).

The *dunce cap*, meanwhile, experienced its own transformation. Although its definitive origins are unknown, one of its earliest appearances was on the heads of heretical prisoners before the Spanish Inquisition. Over the next few hundred years, a tradition emerged of putting struggling students at a separate "dunces' table," followed by pointed hats (often with a capital *D* inscribed) to denote dim-wittedness in classrooms. They were not called "dunce caps" until Charles Dickens's *Old Curiosity Shop* (1840), but by that time they were already the bane of skylarkers and slow learners alike in classrooms the world over.

All of this would surely have broken Scotus's heart, whose intellect was unparalleled in its time. Though he was beatified by Pope John Paul II in 1993, becoming "St. Dunce" was surely cold comfort for the beleaguered Franciscan wunderkind of the high Middle Ages.

⚜ Cooper's ligaments ⚜

n. supportive fibrous structures throughout the breast that partially sheathe the lobes shaping the breast; these ligaments affect the image of the glandular tissue on a mammogram

—*Taber's Cyclopedic Medical Dictionary, Twentieth Edition*

Perhaps no other extraordinary medical career has been reduced more pitifully than that of Sir Astley Paston Cooper. He was the sergeant surgeon to nineteenth-century royalty, was vice president of the Royal Society, and is the unfortunate namesake of the perceived condition of a pendulous bosom perhaps resulting from inadequate undergarment support—the slang term for which is *Cooper's Droop*.

Cooper was born the son of an English clergyman in 1768. He was an exemplary student of anatomy and eventually became a celebrated surgeon, professor, and lecturer. He was an indefatigable researcher and defended both the comparative anatomy lesson of a dissected elephant and the crucial role of resurrectionists (body snatchers) to provide corpses for medical training (see *burke* and *bishop*). He wrote a seminal two-volume treatise on hernias, pioneered work in vascular surgery, removed a royal cyst from the head of King George IV, and was eventually knighted and baroneted.

He was also an authority on mammary glands.

Though he died more than a century before the era of sexual revolution and brassiere tossing, Cooper would likely have warned the newly liberated ladies that the sartorial shackles they were eschewing might help postpone some inevitable sagging (though the jury is still out on whether this is due to gravity or not). Among the myriad anatomical features Cooper identified, studied, and eventually named were the fibrocollagenous septa that attach the breasts to the body. He discovered that, unlike Kegel exercises for the pelvis or sit-ups for a spare tire, there was no treatment to restore elasticity to these ligaments once they were stretched. He believed that even the most pristine mammary profile, if subjected to extended tension, will languish.

Cooper once said, "The means by which I preserve my own health are temperance, early rising, and spunging the body every morning with cold water, a practice I have pursued for thirty years; and though I go from this heated theatre into the squares of the Hospital, in the severest winter nights, with merely silk stockings on my legs, yet I scarcely ever have a cold." Despite these precautions, Cooper died in 1841 in London, and a statue of him was raised in St. Paul's Cathedral. Both in his own time and shortly after, he was further memorialized through street names, public parks, and schools, as well as through a slew of true clinical eponyms, including Cooper's fascia (covering of the spermatic cord), Cooper's testis (testicular neuralgia), and Cooper's hernia, among many others.

The exact date of the first usage of the term *Cooper's Droop* is debatable, but it found new pop-culture life in 1978 through Samuel Shem's satirical novel *The House of God*, in which a young medical intern waxes poetic on his girlfriend's bosom: "Oh, how I love her breasts when she dances. Cooper's ligaments suspend the breasts. Cooper's Droopers, if they stretch."

Unfortunately, despite his venerable contributions to medicine, this snickering and rhyming word coupling is the way he is most widely remembered today.

◅| mesmerize |▻

> *v.* to affect (a person) as if by hypnosis; to fascinate, hold spellbound
>
> —*Oxford English Dictionary*

When we find ourselves mesmerized, perhaps by the champagne-glass shape of a courtesan's bosom (see *pompadour*), we are invoking the memory of Franz Anton Mesmer, an eighteenth-century German physician whose controversial theories formed an early basis for hypnosis.

History cannot quite decide what to make of

Dr. Mesmer—whether he was a quack, a con man, or a visionary. In any case, he was born Friedrich Anton Mesmer in 1734 in Swabia, Germany, and studied medicine at the University of Vienna. The late 1700s were sort of an experimental free-for-all in European medicine. In 1774, Mesmer was able to convince a patient to create an "artificial tide" in her body by swallowing a solution of iron, and then he surrounded her with magnets. Mesmer attributed the "mysterious fluid" she felt coursing through her, and the subsequent relief of her symptoms, not to the effect of the physical magnets but to his own *magnétisme animal*. He was not referring to his powerful mojo. Instead, Mesmer believed in an ethereal medium that existed in animate beings that he could manipulate through animal magnetism, quite separate from mineral magnetism, cosmic magnetism, or planetary magnetism.

Reports vary on how and how well this actually worked. In many cases, Mesmer would hold the thumbs of his patients, sit with his knees touching theirs, and stare into their eyes. For the next few hours he would alternately pass his hands up and down their arms and press on their lower abdomens. Convulsions were common. For those more interested in a group scene, Mesmer could accommodate up to twenty people at a time, all seated around a short vessel (called a *baquet*) studded with iron bars and ropes, allowing each patient to complete the "circuit" and communicate between the *baquet* and the patients as Mesmer conducted his invisible fluid in a collective trance.

This all went on for a number of years, with Mesmer now living in France amid divided opinion on whether he was a charlatan or a great physician. He caused such a stir that Louis XVI convened a French Royal Commission to determine if the supposed magnetic fluid was real. Included in the august group were then ambassador Benjamin Franklin, Antoine "Father of Chemistry" Lavoisier (see also *gibberish*), and physician Joseph-Ignace Guillotin, whom history has inaccurately saddled with the invention of a mechanical death machine (see *guillotine*).

While the commission could not find any evidence for the existence of Mesmer's mystical fluid, they did not dispute the fact that his treatments were effective. Unfortunately for the good doctor, however, they asserted that his cures were more than likely due to the imaginations of his patients. Mesmer was never vindicated, though subsequent "mesmerists" (see *finagle*) developed further techniques for suggestion-induced trances, leading to the development of modern hypnosis in the midnineteenth century, many years after Mesmer died in relative obscurity in 1815.

Though current practitioners would dispute Mesmer's belief that a hypnotic trance is mediated by animal magnetism, some American settlers thought it seemed reasonable. One account for the naming of Mesmerizer Creek, Texas, is that an early resident struck on a novel way to domesticate American bison— through hypnosis.

◅ finagle ▻

v. to use dishonest or devious methods to bring
something about

—Oxford English Dictionary

In a curious etymological footnote to the story of Franz
Anton Mesmer (see *mesmerize*), some have suggested
that German mesmerist Gregor von Feinaigle might
be the source for the word *finagle*. Feinaigle was a priest
turned educator at the turn of the nineteenth century
who developed an elaborate mnemonic system for
remembering absurdly long lists of numbers, in which
digits are converted to consonants and then vowels
added to create visual words.

By all accounts, it was almost impossible for anyone but Feinaigle to achieve. One early experimenter
described it so:

> I saw the moment when I became insane while
> seeking to benefit from the beautiful inventions of
> Mr. Feinaigle. . . . My head was a true chaos.

Feinaigle eventually moved to Dublin, opened a
school for boys founded on his memory techniques,
and then died.

The school closed shortly after.

⊰ Luddite ⊱

n. one who opposes the introduction of new technology, esp. into a place of work

—*Oxford English Dictionary*

Assuming this word's origin is not apocryphal, poor dim-witted and unwitting Ned Ludd has had his name co-opted by protesting textile workers in the nineteenth century and branded on technology skeptics in the twentieth and twenty-first—all because he had one extraordinarily bad day at the office.

Ludd is believed to have lived outside of Leicester in central England in the late 1770s. He was a weaver and, if the legend is true, a bit of a simpleton. One day, in a fit of blind rage (and for motives unknown), Ludd apparently smashed two mechanical knitting machines. These "stocking frames" emulated hand-knitting and were precursors of the large-scale textile machines that would eventually lower the wages and replace the jobs of thousands of British workers over the next half century. In the decades that followed, whenever a piece of equipment was damaged (deliberately or otherwise), British workers would claim that Ned Ludd had done it.

The gritty and dehumanizing Industrial Revolution in the United States was presaged a century earlier in England. Both living and working conditions for laborers declined as technologies were introduced to reduce the need for skilled artisans. Unskilled workers were paid pittance wages to operate new machines, and resentment reached a fever pitch in the early nineteenth century when scattered acts of equipment sabotage gave way to full-scale riots between 1811 and 1816. Starting in Nottingham and eventually spreading all over England, masked workers conducted midnight raids on English factories and systematically wrecked the enormous automated looms that were replacing handicraft and directly threatening their livelihoods. These disaffected and destructive laborers, many of whom were now unemployed, called themselves Luddites in homage to knitter-knocker Ned.

Luddites started warning factory owners that their (imaginary) leader "King Ludd" would take care of their equipment if they did not remove it themselves, and the riots became increasingly violent. Wooden debris was thrown from factory windows to burn in the streets. One factory owner was murdered after calling on soldiers to fire on a protesting mob, killing one of the Luddites. "Machine breaking" became a capital crime in 1812, and dozens of captured protesters were hanged or shipped to prison colonies in Australia over the next several months. The Luddite movement was ultimately quieted by 1817 without having been able to effect any real change in working conditions.

In the late twentieth century, the meaning of *Luddite* shifted away from concerns over the dehumanizing impacts of technology and implied simply a resistance to new things. Laggards to the acceptance of the Internet, cellular phones, and social networking were considered Luddites, as were elderly folks who simply could not be bothered to embrace new gadgetry. However, there has since been a backlash against this anti-Luddite movement. As always-on communications connectivity has permeated evenings, weekends, and quiet moments, many are contemplating the bumper stickers that have started popping up across (of all places) Silicon Valley—"The Luddites Were Right."

⊰ Fourierism ⊱

n. a system for reorganizing society into cooperative communities of small self-sustaining groups
—*Merriam-Webster's Collegiate Dictionary, Eleventh Edition*

Fourierism is a prime example of good intentions paving the road to derision. It is a disheartening shame that a man who introduced the word *feminism*, championed equal rights, and sought only to improve the lot of the world should be remembered as the father of more than forty failed utopias.

Sir Thomas More first coined the term *utopia* in his 1516 book titled, well, *Utopia*, based on the ideal vision of society in Plato's *Republic*. More's imaginary community lived on an imaginary island, and the word itself was formed with Greek roots meaning "no place." More clearly did not believe such a place could actually exist, but others have dared to dream.

François Marie Charles Fourier was born in eastern

France in 1772, and a substantial inheritance from his businessman father enabled him to travel around Europe and explore various merchant and municipal careers before finally settling down as a writer, publishing his first book in 1808. Even in those early writings he revealed his progressive nature, insisting, for example, that society could not advance without extending liberty to women, though he would not describe *féminisme* until 1837, the year of his death.

Fourier believed that societies should be cooperative and primarily agricultural, and his vision for an earthly paradise was to establish communes called "phalanxes" with precisely 1,620 people (2 each of the 810 personalities Fourier theorized were produced by twelve passions imbued in humans) who would live in giant apartment complexes called "phalansteries." Despite the smack of communism, phalanxers were free to choose their careers and paid according to the desirability of their occupations. Workers with the crappiest jobs were the wealthiest and were allowed to live on the top floors of the phalansteries, although everyone would enjoy at least a set minimum wage. It is important to note that Fourier was also convinced that once millions of his communities flourished in a World Congress of Phalanxes, the oceans would turn to lemonade. His followers were a bit of a mixed bag.

While all of this might have been fine for France, it seems unimaginable that this might have sparked interest in the notoriously self-indulgent United States, and yet at least five ultimately failing colonies were established in New York State in the mid-1800s, and a hulking phalanstery building still survives today (sans Fourierists) as a private residence in New Jersey. A similar community established in Utopia, Ohio, in 1844 was destroyed by a flood in 1847, and in 1855, Fourierists founded a commune called La Reunion near Dallas, Texas. The various colonists there were capable weavers, brewers, watchmakers, and storekeepers—but none were proper farmers. A plague of grasshoppers and harsh Texas reality dissolved the commune by 1860.

Fourier was a bright-eyed philosopher whose dreams were perhaps too idealistic for the real world, and his name is invoked today to describe any well-intentioned pipe dream. As philosopher Walter Benjamin wrote, "Only in the summery middle of the nineteenth century, only under its sun, can one conceive of Fourier's fantasy materialized."

Pass the lemonade.

⊲│Nobel Prize│⊳

n. each of six (formerly five) prizes awarded annually to individuals who are judged to have contributed most in the fields of physics, chemistry, physiology or medicine, literature, the promotion of peace, and economics

— *Oxford English Dictionary*

It is hardly notorious to have one's name associated with an internationally recognized award for peace, but it is important to realize that Alfred Nobel bought his legacy of goodwill to avoid a fate similar to that of Joseph-Ignace Guillotin (see *guillotine*). Nobel simply did not want to be remembered as the inventor of dynamite.

Premature obituaries occur more often than one might expect. In 1922 a New York newspaper mistakenly announced, "Pope Benedict XV Is Dead," only to feature a later edition headlined, "Pope Has Remarkable Recovery." In 2003 CNN.com famously leaked in-progress obituaries and templates for numerous celebrities. Fidel Castro's was apparently derived from Ronald Reagan's and described the Cuban leader as a "lifeguard, athlete, movie star," while Dick Cheney's was based on a template from Queen Elizabeth and described him as the "UK's favorite grandmother." Finally, though not technically an obituary, when in 1897 a journalist was sent to ask Mark Twain about his health (mistaking the author with an ill cousin), the humorist later wrote the oft-misquoted comment, "The report of my death is an exaggeration."

But the premature obituary with the greatest lasting impact on humanity is surely that of Alfred Nobel. In 1888 several newspapers mistakenly published his death notice following the passing of his brother Ludvig. One French newspaper used the opportunity to condemn Nobel's invention of dynamite and wrote, "Dr. Alfred Nobel, who became rich by finding ways to kill more people faster than ever before, died yesterday." Nobel was apparently so horrified by his potential legacy that he ultimately rewrote his will in 1895 to dedicate approximately $9 million to establish the Nobel Foundation.

Nobel was born in Stockholm, Sweden, in 1833. Trained as a chemist, Nobel became fascinated with explosives and worked to develop a safe way to handle the recently discovered nitroglycerine, which he combined with rock powder and then sawdust to create Nobel's Blasting Powder (i.e., dynamite). He patented his creation in 1867, did the same for blasting gelatin (gelignite) in 1876, and made a fortune. Just as Guillotin believed his invention would humanize capital punishment (see *guillotine*) and Gatling believed his weapon would reduce military casualties (see *Gatling gun*), Nobel likewise had a naïve faith in humanity's willingness to eliminate human suffering. Though he invented dynamite to be used in construction, he recognized its potential military use and wrote, "My factories may end war sooner than your congresses. The day when two army corps will be able to destroy each other in one second, all civilized nations will recoil away from war in horror and disband their armies."

It is ironic that Nobel's legacy of promoting peace should be born of a newspaper article describing him as a "merchant of death." Perhaps it is then fitting that at least three of the recipients of his prize (philosopher Bertrand Russell, South African president Nelson Mandela, and playwright Harold Pinter) share with him a singularly peculiar distinction—all received premature obituaries.

Typhoid Mary

n. one that is by force of circumstances a center from which something undesirable spreads
    —*Merriam-Webster's Collegiate Dictionary, Eleventh Edition*

When wheezing and sneezing employees show up for work instead of taking an allotted sick day, they are often called a Typhoid Mary—invoking the dead and virulent namesake of hash- and fever-slinging Mary Mallon.

Like many unintentional bacterial gifts, typhoid fever is spread through the intake of food or water contaminated with infected feces (see also *Maginot*). While not typically fatal, it nevertheless plagues its victims with fever, sweating, diarrhea, and furious anger at whoever did not wash up after using the bathroom. The height of its mortality rate in the United States was in the late nineteenth century, just around the time Mary Mallon immigrated to the United States from Ireland.

Mallon was born in 1869, sought her fortune in the New World in 1884, and was well established as a cook in New York City by the turn of the century. However, when members of one of the families who hired her unexpectedly contracted typhoid, they hired civil engineer and typhoid researcher George Soper to investigate. Soper soon discovered that Mallon had sped through seven jobs between 1900 and 1907, leaving a wake of twenty-two typhoid cases and at least one death. Though a complete stranger to her, Soper approached Mallon; suggested she might have typhoid; and requested stool, urine, and blood samples. The Irish cook refused, and the rest is history.

Tensions escalated. Mallon herself did not feel or appear sick and was convinced she was being unfairly targeted as a working-class Irish woman. Soper, meanwhile, returned to question Mallon again, this time with a doctor, followed eventually by a New York City health inspector. Mallon refused them all. She was finally arrested, found to be a carrier for typhoid, and placed in isolation for three years by the board of health. Though Mallon was eventually released with the agreement that she would no longer work as a cook, she soon discovered that work as a laundress or other house servant paid comparatively little, so she assumed a fake name and took a job cooking again in New York's Sloane Hospital for Women. While there, Mallon passed along her special sauce to twenty-five more unwitting victims, one of whom died.

Mallon's identity was eventually discovered, and she was arrested and quarantined again on North Brother Island. By this point, Mallon was known to have infected fifty-three people total (three of whom had died) and was referred to publicly as "Typhoid Mary." Sympathy for her cause had evaporated, and she would spend the rest of her life under quarantine, suffer a paralyzing stroke, and ultimately die six years later of pneumonia in 1938 at the age of sixty-nine.

It has since been theorized that Mallon might have contracted typhoid from her mother before she was born and simply never experienced any symptoms. Though she protested her innocence to the end, an autopsy indicated that Typhoid Mary was still harboring live bacteria in her gallbladder when she died.

Bon appétit.

CHAPTER SIX

Misfits & Misanthropes

⊰{laconic}⊱

adj. short; brief; pithy; sententious; expressing much in few words

—*Webster's New Universal Unabridged Dictionary,*
Second Edition

Our word for tough, no-nonsense speech comes not from one person but from a whole nation of brusque barbarians from ancient Greece—the Laconians.

The wide brushstrokes of grade-school history typically contrast two groups of ancient Greeks—the Athenians and the Spartans. Athenians were the bookish, artsy, democratic ones, while Spartans were the beefy, sporty, slave-driving ones. Laconia was the region of ancient Greece that surrounded the city of Sparta, and all men who were not slaves were expected to be soldiers. There was little tolerance for philosophical or intellectual chitchat, and the Spartans did not wax poetic.

Lycurgus was a central lawgiver of Sparta who famously advocated conscripting boys into the military at the age of seven and insisted (perhaps apocryphally) that no other tools besides a saw and an ax could be used when building a house. He was also the king of the one-liner. When he was offered a proposal to establish a democracy in Sparta, he advised, "Begin with your own family."

Dienekes was a Spartan officer rumored to have been the bravest soldier at the Battle of Thermopylae—made famous to nonclassicists by 1962's *300 Spartans* and Frank Miller's *300*. Sadly, both of those films left Dienekes off the cast list, but they still used his chest-thumping zinger. When he was told the night before the battle that the arrows from the Persian archers would blot out the sun, he replied, "Good. Then we shall fight in the shade."

Before the same battle, King Leonidas was told by Xerxes that the Persian army would spare his vastly outnumbered men if they surrendered their arms, to which he replied, *"Molon labe"*—"Come and take them."

But perhaps the most famous example of the Spartans' concise speech came when Philip II of Macedon (see *philippic*) prepared to invade Laconia. There are many versions of the message Philip supposedly sent:

"If I win this war, you will be slaves forever."

"If I bring my army into your land, I will destroy your farms, slay your people, and raze your city."

There is universal agreement about the ultimate laconic response:

"If."

❧ beggar ❧

n. one who lives by asking alms, or makes it his business to beg for charity

—*Webster's New Universal Unabridged Dictionary,*
Second Edition

Anyone who has ever heard the elaborate and eloquent panhandler pitches on a New York City subway might be surprised to learn that the original word *beggar* most likely comes indirectly from the French word for stammering or stuttering—*bègue*. Tongue-tied twelfth-century Belgian priest Lambert le Bègue (Lambert the Stammerer) began an earnest lay order of nuns and monks that eventually garnered him notoriety as the High Priest of Hobos.

The origin of the word *beggar* (which predates the word *beg*) has plagued etymologists for centuries, having meandered historically through Middle Dutch *beggaert*, Middle English *beggare*, Old French *begard*, and Medieval Latin *beghardi*. But many believe it all started with Father Lambert, who served as a popular parish priest in Liège, Belgium, circa 1150. He established a secular order dedicated to easing the social suffering caused by the

Crusades and soon attracted hundreds of members, who were required to live in communal poverty but could also own private property and get married. The gents became known as *beghardi* or *Beghards* and the ladies became *beghinae* and lived in Beguine convents. (Lest a reader get any strange ideas about what these nuns were doing behind closed doors, the hip-rolling dance called the *beguine* comes from the islands of Martinique and Guadeloupe and is believed to have no relation.)

During his own life, Lambert le Bègue railed against corrupt clergy and was conspicuously outspoken about ordinations that were either purchased (simony) or passed through families (nepotism). He became almost a cult leader, and the secular sons and daughters who believed in his pre-Reformation ideals quickly multiplied and spread across the medieval Low Countries in what are roughly Belgium, Luxembourg, and the Netherlands today. The Beguines were women (predominantly destitute widows of the Crusades) who wanted the perks of sisterhood without the paperwork of monastic vows. They helped the poor and lived quiet lives of good works, only occasionally suffering charges of heresy for their free-spirited ways. Meanwhile, the brotherhood of Beghards was a loose horde of former guilded tradesmen who were often worn out from long careers of labor and sought a limited-commitment religious experience.

While initially living together in monastic cloisters, in the late thirteenth and early fourteenth centuries the Beghards began swarming the countryside, successfully seeking alms for the poor. Sensing a grifting opportunity, soulless imposters began posing as

Beghards and taking advantage of those believing they were supporting the less fortunate. Soon variations on the word *Beghard* were popping up all over Europe to represent wandering mendicants.

As for the original Beghard, Lambert le Bègue was eventually condemned and imprisoned for heresy (despite direct appeals to the pope) but managed to escape and live out his life in Liège, where he died in 1177. He never lived to see his spiritual philosophy (and speech impediment) transform into its indigent incarnation.

⊰ Neanderthal ⊱

n. one who suggests a caveman in appearance, mentality, or behavior
—*Merriam-Webster's Collegiate Dictionary, Eleventh Edition*

In 1680, the same year he died, Joachim Neander wrote the concluding stanza of one of his most beloved hymns, "Heaven and Earth and Sea and Air."

> *Lord, great wonders workest Thou!*
> *To Thy sway all creatures bow;*
> *Write Thou deeply in my heart*
> *What I am, and what Thou art.*

Neander was a thoughtful schoolteacher, minister, and poet, still honored two centuries after his death by having the Neander Valley (the *Neander Thal*) near Düsseldorf named for him. Unfortunately, just a few decades later, the first complete skeleton of what was initially believed to be an early humanoid group of unintelligent brutes was discovered in his valley, and his legacy has never been the same.

The gentle theologian was born in Bremen, Germany, in 1650, though his grandfather's surname had been Neumann. Two generations earlier, fashionable Germans wanting to demonstrate their love and support for the nation's renaissance of education translated their names into classical Greek—thus, Neumann ("new man") became Neander. Neander studied theology and taught Latin (as his father had) in Düsseldorf all through his twenties, and it was during this bucolic period that Neander meandered through the nearby limestone canyon, whose rocks and rills enveloped the Düssel River and provided the inspiration for his more than sixty hymns. Neander died of tuberculosis (some believe the plague) in 1680 at the tender age of thirty.

In the early nineteenth century, a portion of the valley he adored was renamed Neandershöhle (Neander's Hole or Hollow), and the entire area became the Neanderthal (Neander Valley) after 1850, with the spelling changed to Neandertal in 1901. As heartwarming as this is, in the years following Neander's death, the verdant dale succumbed to industrial limestone excavating. In 1856, miners discovered what they thought were bear bones in a cliff cave on their quarry site. After investigation by local naturalist Johann Fuhlrott and confirmation from anatomy professor Hermann

Schaaffhausen at the University of Bonn, the skeleton pieces were announced to be ancient human remains and estimated to be tens of thousands of years old.

The reports were initially met with skepticism because Bible thumpers still held sway, and Charles Darwin's equally heretical *On the Origin of Species* would not be published for three more years. Objections aside, the skullcap, thigh, arm, and rib bones were dubbed "Neanderthal Man" in 1863. It was later discovered that similar skulls had been found in Belgium and Gibraltar several years prior, but the existing attribution to Neander still held.

The large bone structure and hulking cranium led many people to assume that this extinct branch of the human tree was composed of dim-witted mouth-breathers, though this has been largely debunked in recent years. Nevertheless, poor Neander's namesake was first cited as a derogatory term as early as 1928 in the *Oxford English Dictionary*. This, no doubt, would have deeply saddened the German hymnist.

> *See how He hath everywhere*
> *Made this earth so rich and fair;*
> *Hill and vale and fruitful land,*
> *All things living show His hand.*

May *his* bones rest in peace.

❦ grangerism ❦

n. the practice of using illustrations taken from a
number of books to illustrate a work
> —*Webster's New Universal Unabridged Dictionary,*
> *Second Edition*

It may be hard to decide whether the Reverend James
Granger should be vilified by history for being the first
to institutionalize illustrative theft from rare sources or
for effectively inventing scrapbooking.

As anyone in illustrated book publishing knows,
securing the usage rights for drawings or photographs is
one of the most tedious but necessary parts of the process, while printing them in full color is one of the most
expensive. James Granger essentially sidestepped both of
these technicalities in 1769 when he published his *Biographical History of England.*

The full title is actually far more absurd and ran
the entire length of a page in progressively smaller and
smaller typeface:

A
BIOGRAPHICAL HISTORY
OF
ENGLAND,
from Egbert the Great to the Revolution:

CONSISTING OF
CHARACTERS DISPOSED IN DIFFERENT CLASSES,

AND ADAPTED TO
A METHODICAL CATALOGUE OF ENGRAVED BRITISH HEADS:

INTENDED AS
AN ESSAY TOWARDS REDUCING
OUR BIOGRAPHY TO SYSTEM,
AND A HELP TO THE KNOWLEDGE OF PORTRAITS:

INTERSPERSED WITH
A VARIETY OF ANECDOTES,
AND
MEMOIRS OF A GREAT NUMBER OF PERSONS,

NOT TO BE FOUND IN ANY OTHER
BIOGRAPHICAL WORK.
WITH A PREFACE,
SHEWING THE UTILITY OF A COLLECTION
OF ENGRAVED PORTRAITS TO SUPPLY THE DEFECT,
AND ANSWER THE VARIOUS PURPOSES, OF MEDALS.

BY THE REV. J. GRANGER,
VICAR OF SHIPLAKE, IN OXFORDSHIRE.

Animum pictura pascit inani.—VIRG.
Celebrare domestica facta.—HOR.

What set the vicar's work apart from other history books of the time was that it was extraordinarily illustrated. What made it historically criminal is that Granger personally clipped more than fourteen thousand engraved portraits from other rare books and private collections to fill his pages. While the 1769 edition had only two volumes, subsequent editions had as many as six, and blank pages were added for readers to mutilate their own libraries' collections and add to the "work." Granger essentially sanctified this behavior by suggesting in his preface that such enhancements by readers might make their own editions more valuable, which indeed they did.

In a chilling vision of crafting to come, so many thousands of people personalized their own editions of *A Biographical History of England* with pillaged engravings—a practice euphemistically known as "extra-illustration"—that librarians, book dealers, and concerned citizens coined the term *grangerism* or *grangerizing* to describe the destructive hobby.

❧ bowdlerize ❧

> *v.* to expurgate (a book or writing), by omitting or modifying words or passages considered indelicate or offensive; to castrate
>
> —*Oxford English Dictionary*

The seemingly well-intentioned Thomas Bowdler has been treated somewhat harshly by history. He has been placed among the ranks of hysterical censors, do-gooders, and fussbudgets (see *Comstockery*) when all he really wanted was to give his children a little more Bard with a little less bawd.

Thomas Bowdler was born in 1754 with a sterling pedigree. His great-grandfather founded the library at Trinity College in Dublin, his grandfather served with Samuel Pepys in the Admiralty, and his father married a wealthy baroness, ensuring the family's financial comfort. When Bowdler was a child, his father gave family readings from the works of Shakespeare, though secretly omitting passages he felt were indelicate for fairer and younger ears. Bowdler was convinced that other parents might also like to share the Bard's work with their families but lacked the improvisational talents of his father. So after retiring from a career in medicine, and with the help of his sister, Henrietta, Bowdler set out to sanitize Shakespeare for a delicate populace.

In 1807, Thomas and Henrietta published the first four volumes of the wholesome *Family Shakespeare*, containing twenty-four of the playwright's works. Bowdler would complete the entire catalogue by 1818. It is only fair to note here that unlike a number of other editors at the time with their vanity projects, Bowdler added nothing to the text. However, the title page clearly announced that "those expressions are omitted which cannot with propriety be read aloud in a family," in addition to "whatever is unfit to be read by a gentleman in a company of ladies."

Bowdler was a devoted reader of Shakespeare but unapologetically wrote that "many words and expressions occur which are of so indecent a nature as to render it highly desirable that they should be erased." Therefore, gone from *Romeo and Juliet* went its pricks and spreading curtains, while *Othello* lost its reference to the "old black ram . . . tupping your white ewe." Meanwhile, Lady Macbeth's "damned" spot turned "crimson," and poor Ophelia's watery suicide in *Hamlet* became an accidental drowning. Though reviled by critics for its literary castrations, *Family Shakespeare* was a fantastic success and reprinted many times over.

Unfortunately for Bowdler, subsequent revisions to other works proved less successful. He died just a few years later, in 1825, and within a decade, his name was being used pejoratively to represent any prudish editing. However, despite the negative connotations with his name, he is not universally castigated. Nineteenth-century poet and Shakespeare scholar Algernon Charles Swinburne famously asserted that "No man ever did better service to Shakespeare than the man who made it possible to put him into the hands of intelligent and imaginative children." Further, many others were eager to come forth and expand his work. Even the venerable Lewis Carroll allegedly had designs for his own expurgation and said, "I have a dream of Bowdlerising Bowdler" and producing a volume of Shakespeare specifically fit for young girls.

Carroll's book was never published, Bowdler was henceforth associated with hypersensitive pruning, and, thanks to modern acceptance of literary integrity, children today can still appreciate Desdemona and Othello "making the beast with two backs."

◦{ spoonerism }◦

n. an accidental transposition of the initial sounds,
or other parts, of two or more words

— *Oxford English Dictionary*

William Archibald Spooner is the Mr. Magoo of notorious namesakes. He was a short, large-headed albino
with poor eyesight whose mangling of words plagued
him for life. His notable quotables (which, in all likeli-
hood, were never uttered by him) run the gamut from
religion ("the Lord is a shoving leopard") to politics
(referring to Her Majesty as "the queer old Dean") to
etiquette ("it is kisstumary to cuss the bride") to philosophy ("We all know what it is to have a half-warmed
fish inside us").

Spooner was born in London in 1844 and spent
most of his career and life at New College, Oxford, as
everything from an undergraduate to a lecturer, dean,
and warden. He also became a priest in the Church of
England in 1875. Spooner himself only ever acknowledged botching the title of a congregational hymn as
"Kinkering Congs Their Titles Take" instead of "Conquering Kings Their Titles Take," though the *Oxford
Dictionary of Quotations* also insists he once opined that
"the weight of rages will press hard upon the employer."
So whence come the slew of spoonerisms we know
and love today? It seems, in part, that crafting and
attributing them to their dean was popular word sport
for students at Oxford in the late nineteenth century,

leading to a host of wordplay witticisms that have been associated with the good reverend ever since.

Linguists refer to phoneme reversal as *metathesis*, and it is far more ubiquitous in English than one might think, with results ranging from the adorable to the infuriating—both a child's pronunciation of "spaghetti" as "pasghetti" and former president George W. Bush's "nucular" instead of "nuclear" are prime examples. "Axing" questions, calling in the "calvary," and admiring "purty" fall "foilage" are some of the most common speech errors in our language, and they often lead to new spellings and pronunciations—dirt was once "drit," and birds were once "bryds."

It is possible that Spooner was not the first person to suffer from public association with the linguistic affliction. Similar tongue twists were first called "marrowskis," believed by some (though the evidence is quite thin) to be based on the speech pattern of Count Joseph Boruwlaski, a Polish-born dwarf who toured the royal courts of Europe in the late eighteenth century as a respectable violinist. Nevertheless, the term *spoonerism* was bandied about at Oxford by 1885 and across all of England by 1900. Spooner himself seemed to have spurned the association early in his life—he once allegedly chastised an expectant crowd by accusing them, "You haven't come for my lecture but just want to hear one of those . . . things"—but came to terms with his legacy by his death in 1930, at the age of eighty-six.

It is somewhat widely acknowledged today that most of Spooner's attributions are apocryphal and should be taken with a few grains of salt. So what would Spooner himself have done with this salt? Apparently he was once dining when a small amount of it was spilled on the table. Mentally reversing the technique for removing a stain, Spooner promptly poured wine on it.

❧ Comstockery ❧

n. zealous suppression of plays, books, etc., considered offensive or dangerous to public morals
—*Webster's New Universal Unabridged Dictionary,*
Second Edition

Anthony Comstock was the American incarnation of Britain's Thomas Bowdler (see *bowdlerize*), and it was none other than famed playwright George Bernard Shaw who immortalized this moral zealot's priggery when he wrote, "Comstockery is the world's standing joke at the expense of the United States. Europe likes to hear of such things. It confirms the deep-seated conviction of the Old World that America is a provincial place, a second-rate country-town civilization after all."

In 1844, many years before the Village People convinced a 1970s generation that it was fun to stay there, the Young Men's Christian Association (YMCA) was founded in London to give factory workers an alternative to a sinful life on the street. It provided prayer and Bible study to improve "the spiritual condition of young men engaged in the drapery and other trades."

It was also the same year that Anthony Comstock was born. Two decades later, after serving in the American Civil War, Comstock worked in the New York City YMCA before launching a Victorian crusade against birth control and what he deemed to be obscene literature.

In 1873 a politically savvy Comstock conceived the New York Society for the Suppression of Vice and persuaded Congress to enact the Comstock Act, a federal law that criminalized sending "obscene, lewd, and/or lascivious" materials through the mail—which included not only pornography but also contraceptive "equipment" and advertisements as well as anatomy textbooks. For his definition of obscenity, Comstock relied on the standard set by the unfortunately (or aptly) named Lord Cockburn in England five years earlier. In 1868, Lord Chief Justice Alexander James Edmund Cockburn defined as obscene materials those that "deprave and corrupt those whose minds are open to such immoral influence." Inspired by Cockburn's articulations, Comstock soon became an armed U.S. Postal Inspector, conducted raids on bookstores, prosecuted more than 3,500 people, and destroyed more than 160 tons of allegedly obscene material.

Comstock attacked George Bernard Shaw's play *Mrs. Warren's Profession* in 1905 and referred to Shaw as an "Irish smut dealer," to which Shaw responded with his now famous comment (quoted above), forever linking Comstock's name with bigoted censorship. Not to be outdone, Comstock embraced the term and described it as "the applying of the noblest principles of law . . . in the interest of Public Morals, especially those of the young." Referring to himself as a "weeder in God's garden," Comstock referred to his liberal targets as "long-haired men and short-haired women" and boasted that his prosecutions had driven at least fifteen people to commit suicide.

One hilariously titled chapter of the Comstock chronicles, however, involved a confiscated shipment of contraceptives from Japan to New York City in 1932. The slightly ribald case of *United States v. One Package of Japanese Pessaries* (diaphragms) in the U.S. Court of Appeals directly confronted the standing prohibition against importing or mailing birth control. It had been these laws that led to the decidedly not hilarious multiple arrests of Planned Parenthood founder (and coiner of the term *birth control*) Margaret Sanger. The ban on contraceptives was eventually declared unconstitutional, but many other portions of the Comstock Act still stand today.

Anthony Comstock died in 1915. Lawyer, author, and free-speech activist Theodore Schroeder later railed that Comstock "stood at the mouth of a sewer, searching for and devouring obscenity for a salary." It is perhaps fitting that the encyclopedic collection of pornography currently owned by the Library of Congress was established with contraband confiscated under the Comstock Act of 1873.

ᵈ⟨ brodie ⟩ᵉ

n. a total failure; fiasco

v. to commit suicide, esp. by jumping from a high place

—*New Dictionary of American Slang*

The largely theatrical slang term for a dramatic flop started out as a pop culture attempted-suicide reference to Steve Brodie, who claimed in 1886 to have jumped off the Brooklyn Bridge and survived.

After thirteen years, the incapacitation of its original builder, and more than two dozen fatalities during its construction, the Brooklyn Bridge finally opened to great fanfare in 1883—at the time, the longest suspension bridge in the world, its towers the tallest in the Western Hemisphere. Unfortunately, a rumor of collapse a week after its opening led to a human stampede and the trampling deaths of a dozen visitors, leaving many wondering if the bridge was, in fact, safe. Master showman P. T. Barnum sought to allay the fears of the public and garner some spectacular publicity by leading a parade of twenty-one elephants (including the show-stopping Jumbo) across the bridge in 1884—thus demonstrating both the structural integrity of the bridge and its potential as a high-profile stage for daredevils and fools.

The first recorded stunt jump from the bridge came in 1885 when Robert E. Odlum leaped from the bridge in a bright red swimsuit, hit the water slightly out of position, and died shortly after from internal injuries. Steve Brodie's claim to fame is slightly more controversial. Some accounts suggest that Brodie was a bartender who offered to take a bridge plunge to settle a barroom bet. Others insist he was a bookmaker from Brooklyn who just wanted publicity. In any case, everyone agrees that Brodie, twenty-three years old at the time, claimed to have jumped off the bridge and survived on July 23, 1886. The only eyewitnesses to his actual "jump" were friends, though many were present to see him fished from the river and arrested for endangering his own life—despite the fact that suicide was not his intent. His fame and notoriety encouraged a parade of jumpers to follow. The first confirmed suicide attempt was in 1892, around the time the daredevil jumps began to taper off.

Though he died in 1901, Brodie's fame lingered through the middle of the twentieth century. Owing to the possible hoax of his jump, bookies began using his name to denote a false fall in boxing; theater patrons used it for any show with high expectations that flopped; and the general public referred to any suicide by jumping, particularly a failed one, as "doing a brodie." His story was featured in the 1933 film *The Bowery*, and a madness-inducing Bugs Bunny drove a fictionalized caricature of him to jump off the Brooklyn Bridge in 1949's *Bowery Bugs*.

There is a (perhaps apocryphal) story that the father of famed boxer Gentleman Jim Corbett was delighted to meet Brodie, whom he identified as the man who had jumped *over* the Brooklyn Bridge. When Brodie corrected him by saying he had jumped *off* of it, the disappointed elder Corbett replied, "Any damn fool can jump *off* it."

❧ Gordon Bennett(!) ❧

int. expressing surprise, incredulity, or exasperation
— *Oxford English Dictionary*

Gordon Bennett is the only historical figure mentioned in this book who also once had an entry in the *Guinness Book of World Records*. He has the dubious distinction of committing the Greatest Engagement Faux Pas for drunkenly urinating in the fireplace belonging to his fiancée's parents. Despite being a Yank, his name has been invoked by Brits for years as an alternative interjection to the slightly sacrilegious "gorblimey!" contraction of "God blind me!"

James Gordon Bennett Jr. was the son of newspaper magnate James Gordon Bennett Sr. In 1835, the elder Bennett founded the infamous New York Herald, which practiced what journalist and critic H. L. Mencken called "journalism for the frankly ignorant and vulgar," and Bennett openly admitted that he felt the role of his publication was "not to instruct but to startle." Its sensational headlines and publicity stunts gave it the leading circulation of its day, but it was the junior Bennett (who was called simply Gordon) who took the paper to new highs (and lows), in perfect keeping with his outrageous lifestyle.

Born in 1841, Bennett spent most of his childhood in France but took over the running of the American paper in 1866. He quickly proved himself to be an equal showman to his father by hiring journalist and adventurer Henry Morton Stanley to find missionary and explorer David Livingstone, who had disappeared in Africa searching for the elusive source of the Nile River. Stanley's exciting dispatches made the Herald's circulation skyrocket, culminating with his fantastic discovery of the pneumonia-, cholera-, and ulcer-ridden Livingstone near Lake Tanganyika and his now infamous introduction, "Dr. Livingstone, I presume?" Bennett had decidedly less geographical success (but, again, increased his circulation) after funding the tragic North Pole expedition of George W. DeLong, who starved, along with nineteen of his crew, while trying to navigate the Bering Strait.

As a newspaper mogul, Bennett lived the opulent life of an international playboy and high-society sportsman. He won the first yacht race across the Atlantic Ocean in 1866, founded the first polo club in the United States in 1876, and established the first and oldest (and still flying) gas balloon race in 1906—the Gordon Bennett Cup in ballooning. He allegedly whipped the white tablecloths off the tables of other diners when he entered restaurants and caused a social scandal when he ruined his engagement with New York socialite Caroline May by entering her family's mansion drunk and then relieving himself in their fireplace. He moved permanently to Paris in 1877, launched the *Paris Herald*, and (somewhat less successfully) ran his now-international newspaper operations primarily by telegram sent from aboard his yacht, the *Lysistrata*.

In 1914, at the age of seventy-three, he married the Baroness de Reuter, widowed daughter-in-law of Paul Reuter, the founder of Reuters news agency. Bennett died four years later and was buried in France. His legacy is a peculiar one. His American newspaper ultimately went out of business, but the *Washington Post* and the *New York Times* reincarnated its European version as the *International Herald Tribune*. He has streets named for him in Paris, has a statue erected in his paper's Herald Square in New York City, and since 1869 has represented the highest award for heroism a New York firefighter can receive—the James Gordon Bennett Medal.

But, most strangely, though he never worked or lived in England, since the early 1930s its inhabitants have exclaimed "Gordon Bennett!" to express tasteful shock. Beyond his flamboyant international lifestyle and newsworthy notoriety, its origin is a mystery.

Gorblimey!

❧⟨Rachmanism⟩❧

> *n.* the exploitation and intimidation of tenants by unscrupulous landlords
>
> —*Oxford English Dictionary*

In the more than forty countries around the world that allow them, rent controls on apartments are generally revered as a boon by tenants and reviled as a bane by landlords. Intended, in part, to keep housing affordable for fixed-income residents, rent controls sometimes lead to despicable behavior by landlords. Choosing slum landlordship as a career should be cause enough for notoriety, but establishing yourself as one of the worst in history requires an extraordinary feat of scumbaggery. Meet Peter Rachman.

Rachman was born in Poland and served time in both German and Soviet labor camps during World War II before fighting alongside the Allies and eventually establishing residency in London in 1948. Described later by one journalist as a classic James Bond villain—"short and fat, with grotesquely tiny hands and feet, he had no neck, a bald head shaped like a soccer ball"—Rachman quickly made a name for himself as a slumlord extraordinaire. In the early 1950s, he began buying rental housing that was inexpensive due to the limited income derived from its rent-controlled units. Rachman would then rent an available room to recent immigrants from the West Indies and encourage them to carouse all night, urinate in public areas, and generally make life as unpleasant as possible for the mostly white tenants living in the neighboring fixed-rent units. Once the sitting tenants were driven out, Rachman could, by law, charge the incoming immigrants as much as he wanted. He was extraordinarily savvy, managed to avoid paying any personal income tax despite owning upwards of five hundred buildings, and was driving a Rolls-Royce in less than a decade.

The immigrants coming to London at that time had few options for housing, and Rachman exploited one and all. He would pack as many tenants into his shabby buildings as the market would bear, and he was particularly fond of converting unused cellar space into prostitution havens. The pudgy landlord was a notorious womanizer who, at one point, kept two of his mistresses in one of his properties in Marylebone. The mistresses ended up at the center of a political scandal involving then secretary of war John Profumo in Prime Minister Harold Macmillan's conservative government. In what became known as "the Profumo affair," the secretary eventually resigned in 1963 after it surfaced that he had been diddling a topless showgirl who was also consorting with a known Russian spy (in addition to being a former lover of Rachman's).

As for Rachman himself, he died of a heart attack at the age of forty-two, just one year before the Profumo story broke. His connection to the scandal brought new attention to his wheelings and dealings and led one political champion of improved housing conditions to coin the term *Rachmanism* to represent all of the reprobate landlords operating in London. Though there were rumors that Rachman had faked his death to avoid possible prosecution, Scotland Yard insists that he is buried in an unmarked grave in a Hertfordshire cemetery.

CHAPTER SEVEN

Politics & Government

⊰{ philippic }⊱

n. a discourse or declaration full of bitter condemna-
tion; a tirade

—*Merriam-Webster's Collegiate Dictionary, Eleventh Edition*

The word for an unbridled and unmitigated verbal
thrashing is the namesake of Philip of Macedon, who
took such an oratorical beating from Greek statesman
Demosthenes that people are still talking about it
more than two thousand years later.

Philip II was born into royalty in the ancient Greek
kingdom of Macedon in 382 BC. He was primed from
birth to be a leader, and the early deaths of his two
older brothers allowed him to ascend to the throne
when he was just twenty-three. He was a spectacular
military leader who greatly extended the Macedonian

kingdom, eventually conquering Athens and inciting a vocal minority of orators to rail against his intrusions.

The most eloquent of his critics was Athenian lawyer and speechwriter Demosthenes, who was born in 384 BC and spent the entire latter half of his life trying to thwart the foreign conquest of the Greek states. Demosthenes allegedly once said of Philip that he was "not only no Greek, nor related to the Greeks, not even a barbarian from any place that can be named with honors, but a pestilent knave from Macedonia." Starting in 351 BC, Demosthenes embarked on a series of three great oratories, known within his lifetime as the "Philippics," denouncing the Macedonian king and imploring his countrymen to stand up for themselves.

What is most remarkable about these lyrical smackdowns is that they were equally attacks on the Greek people themselves for allowing Philip to deceive and abuse them. Also, unlike modern, sound bite–savvy commentators who rely on zinging one-liners, Demosthenes was the master of the exhaustive, pile-driving pillory. His rhetorical assaults on Philip were neither sarcastic nor hyperbolic. They were methodical and unassailable arguments crafted to convince an apathetic populace to abandon the status quo. "I believe [that] Philip is intoxicated with the magnitude of his exploits . . . openly fleecing and pillaging the Greeks, one after another, attacking and enslaving their cities."

Sadly for Demosthenes and his fellow citizens, Philip ultimately succeeded in subsuming Athens—though he was not so successful with neighboring Sparta (see *laconic*). He fathered Alexander the Great, who assumed his throne after Philip's assassination by one of his bodyguards in 336 BC. Though Demosthenes would eventually outlive both father and son, in 322 BC the mighty orator took his own life by chewing on the tip of a poisoned quill to avoid arrest for treason by Alexander's successor. Despite his failure to stem the tide of the Macedonian onslaught, Demosthenes was never forgotten, and his Philippics have been memorized and recited by aspiring orators for generations. Even more than three hundred years later, Cicero similarly eviscerated Mark Antony, basing his invectives on the speeches of Demosthenes and earning them the title of "Philippics" as well.

The honors for Philip's shameful eponym will forever belong to Demosthenes, who would surely be delighted by their staying power. Plutarch once wrote that when Demosthenes heard that Philip had been praised for being eloquent, attractive, and an excellent drinking companion, he quipped that those three traits were suitable qualifications for a rhetorician, a woman, and a sponge, respectively—but not a prince.

Zing!

⋖ Machiavellian ⋗

adj. of, relating to, or characteristic of Machiavelli, or of his principles or alleged principles; practicing, or

characterized by, (esp. political) expediency; unscrupulous, duplicitous; astute, cunning, scheming

—*Oxford English Dictionary*

Unlike Joseph McCarthy (see *McCarthyism*), who was almost certainly and inescapably evil, the man best remembered for advising that it is better to be feared than loved was a thoughtful philosopher doomed to be associated forever with the harsh and cruel advice of his most cynical work.

Born in Florence in 1469, Niccolò di Bernardo dei Machiavelli was a Renaissance man in the truest sense of the term. His legacy is as a philosopher and political scientist, but he was equally a civil servant, poet, and musician. He became a Florentine ambassador and diplomat in his twenties and thirties but ultimately proved to be on the losing side of Florence's resistance to the treacherous Medici family. He was deposed, arrested, and even suffered torture by strappado (hung by his wrists, bound behind his back, to dislocate his shoulders) before finally being released. It was after his time in prison that he penned the political treatise that would make him famous.

Though he also wrote plays, novels, and poems, Machiavelli's most inflammatory work is undoubtedly *The Prince*, in which he advises a fictitious new ruler on how best to rule a kingdom. He argues that a ruler can and should use any means necessary to establish order and maintain power. The politically slimy element of this theory is that it suggests that a leader should outwardly appear just and moral while inwardly permitting cruel and merciless governance to preserve the state. Violence and deceit are simply necessary means to a successful political end. Though he wrote it in 1513, like nearly all of his works it was not published for nearly two decades—five years after Machiavelli died.

The work has always provided fodder for debate, but many world leaders have turned to Machiavelli for inspiration and rationalization for their activities. Both Napoleon and Mussolini wrote extensively about *The Prince*, and Stalin supposedly kept a copy by his bed. The same may not be said of all of his books. For example, modern politicians seeking dating tips from one of his many lesser-known works, *The Golden Ass* (*L'asino d'oro*), are likely to be disappointed as it is a satirical poem and not a political primer on philandering.

Machiavelli's name was not used pejoratively until well after his death in 1527. In fact the epitaph on his monument in Florence waxes, "For so great a name, no praise is adequate." Within fifty years, however, a fair portion of that reverence had turned to revulsion. The initial use of his namesake to represent cunning governance eventually morphed, likely unfairly, into actions intended for personal gain. While many modern scholars insist that *The Prince* and his other controversial works do not represent his personal beliefs, it is difficult not to feel that at least some of Machiavelli's notoriety is self-imposed and deserved. He wrote in *The Prince* that people "are ungrateful, fickle, liars, and deceivers."

Suit yourself, Nick.

❧ tontine ❧

n. a joint arrangement whereby the participants usu.
contribute equally to a prize that is awarded entirely
to the participant who survives all the others

—*Merriam-Webster's Collegiate Dictionary, Eleventh Edition*

Despite devising an investment scheme that has been
the fodder for countless murder-mystery plots, comedies,
television series, and even a proposed game show, precious little is known about the life and times of Lorenzo
Tonti—governor, banker, and inventor of the tontine.

As would be the case again one hundred years later
under Louis XV (see *silhouette*), France was in serious
financial trouble in 1653 under Louis XIV, and one
ingenious solution to help replenish the Sun King's
royal coffers came from an Italian banker who advocated
gambling on the deaths of investors. More specifically,
Lorenzo Tonti proposed establishing an investment that
would pay regular interest dividends to all those who
committed to lifelong participation, with individual
dividend amounts increasing as participants died off.
The lone survivor would get all of the remaining interest, while the state would receive the entire principal.

The French parliament was a bit squirmy about
embracing a plan whose success hinged on the early
deaths of its participants, but they eventually got over
it. The first French tontine finally appeared in 1689,
more than five years after Tonti's death, and cost
around $1,500 in modern currency to join. Forty years

later, the final survivor pocketed more than $360,000 in dividends, with France keeping all of the principal. It was not precisely a get-rich-quick scheme, but it worked well enough to be duplicated across Europe and even in America. Perhaps ironically, the first tontines issued in England in 1693 were used to fund its part of the Nine Years' War against France. Meanwhile, tontines in the United States were often used to fund construction projects, with the Tontine Coffee House on Wall Street becoming the early home for the New York Stock Exchange. In the following century, all manner of exploitation emerged. The shrewd began buying tontines for very young children, leading to quick returns for investors and long returns for governments. Bogus, nongovernmental schemes began popping up everywhere, and mysterious and premature deaths of investors became commonplace.

Though hardly comical in real life, these latter occurrences were eventually lampooned in multiple mediums. Robert Louis Stevenson's novel (and its 1966 film) *The Wrong Box* featured two brothers as the last survivors of a seventy-year tontine—one trying to kill the other—with black-comedy results. P. G. Wodehouse expanded the tontine theme in his novel *Something Fishy* by making the final payment go to the last investor's son to remain unmarried. Tontine plots have run the television spectrum, from *Bugs Bunny* and *The Wild Wild West* to *Barney Miller* and *M*A*S*H*, including an action-packed senior-citizen speedboat fight in the "Curse of the Flying Hellfish" episode of *The Simpsons*. In 2008, there were even plans for a reality television game show in which contestants would invest their life savings and then compete across seven continents for a grand prize of $10 million.

For many, however, these plotlines must remain the stuff of fiction. After a few too many suspicious subscriber deaths during their heyday of the eighteenth and nineteenth centuries, tontines have since been banned in the United States and Britain. Though never part of one of his own schemes, Tonti died in 1684 of unknown causes.

⊲ silhouette ⊳

n. a portrait obtained by tracing the outline of a profile, head, or figure by means of its shadow or in some other way, and filling in the whole with black
— *Oxford English Dictionary*

Financing an expensive and unpopular foreign conflict has never been an easy task, and in mid-eighteenth-century France, it fell upon the namesake of those familiar black profile cutouts—Étienne de Silhouette, the hapless and penny-pinching French controller general of finances under Louis XV.

Starting in 1754, France began waging the Seven Years' War against England. Truth be told, the unpleasantness lasted ten years and was called the French and Indian War in North America and the War of the

Conquest in French Canada—but no matter the name, it was an expensive proposition, and King Louis XV needed someone to pull off a monetary miracle.

Much to the disgust of most of the French nobility, one of Louis' chief advisers was his bouffanted mistress—Madame de Pompadour (see *pompadour*). After catching a free moment from appointing window treatments, she recommended her good friend Monsieur Silhouette to help reduce the skyrocketing deficit and replenish the French war chest.

Born Étienne de Silhouette in 1709, the fifty-year-old financier seemed a strange choice to solve France's fiscal concerns, as he had studied finance and economics in London and was an unapologetic Anglophile, having translated multiple works by Alexander Pope, Henry Bolingbroke, and William Warburton into French. But Madame de Pompadour had Louis XV's ear, among other things, and was able to secure him the position of controller general in 1759.

It is reported that he saved the French treasury 72 million francs in his first twenty-four hours in power—all at the expense of the rich and privileged. He almost immediately confirmed the worst fears of his noble detractors when he placed a land tax on large estates and reduced the pensions of the wealthiest Frenchmen. One would think that all of this populism would have made him a hero among the hoi polloi, but cartoons and jokes began to abound at all levels of society, poking fun at Silhouette's hopeless attempts to overcome a crippling deficit. He began taxing all external signs of wealth—luxury goods, decorative windows and doors, servants, and farms. Unable to raise enough money through these new taxes, he then turned to the dining room and insisted that French gold and silver (especially the plates and tableware of Louis XV) be cast into the melting pot. This proved to be the last straw for his enemies, and Silhouette was finally forced to abandon his post after only eight months in office.

Soon, any cheaply manufactured bauble was said to be made *á la Silhouette*, though the man's connection to the inexpensive art form is less clear. The foremost theory is that his name became synonymous with what the English at the time called "shades" simply because the paper profiles were a cheap alternative to the expensive portraits or sculptures commissioned by nobility. They thus became the preferred medium of a citizenry suffering under Silhouette's heavy taxation.

Despite this negative connotation, silhouettes spread to the New World and were hugely popular in America from 1790 to 1840, after which point they were overshadowed by the invention of the camera. They had a bit of a pop culture renaissance in the 1950s through the opening credits of *Alfred Hitchcock Presents* and then the James Bond film series, finally cementing their cachet of cool in the early iPod commercials.

One competing theory surrounding Silhouette's namesake is that he brought the association upon himself. After leaving office in disgrace in 1759, Silhouette quietly retired to his estate at Bry sur Marne and purportedly pursued one of his favorite pastimes—cutting out black paper profiles of his family—until his candle was extinguished in 1767.

❧ Potemkin ❧

adj. sham, insubstantial; consisting of little or nothing behind an impressive facade
— *Oxford English Dictionary*

Anyone trying to sell a house should know the subtle
tricks for sprucing up a shabby property—toothpaste
for wall cracks, shoe polish for hardwood scratches, and
fresh-baked cookies to mask the odor of incontinent pets.
Some scholars believe (although the historical record is
sparse and there is ample evidence to the contrary) that
Grigory Potemkin may have pulled the greatest bait and
switch in history when he built entire bogus villages in
the arid wasteland of southwestern Ukraine to impress
his boss and sugar mama—Catherine the Great.

Potemkin was born to a military family along the
Dnieper River in western Russia in 1739. He would
eventually be part of the 1762 coup that overthrew
the hapless Peter III and put Peter's opportunistic
wife, Catherine II (soon to be "Great"), on the throne,
ushering in a new era of sex and statesmanship that
would last for more than thirty years. Catherine liber-
ally commingled her public and private lives, vocally
proclaiming that she and Peter had never consummated their marriage (despite the existence of their
"son," Paul) and enjoying affairs with multiple advisers
and supporters—though, strangely and ironically, *not*
one of the most legendary philanderers of the age (see
Casanova). Catherine called on Potemkin for military

guidance when her crown was threatened in the early 1770s, and the two inevitably became lovers.

Within a decade, the flagging powers of the Ottoman Empire (see *ottoman*) and others ceded control of an enormous swath of land, almost a quarter of a million square miles, to Russia as Catherine expanded her empire ever south and west. Catherine named Potemkin a prince of the Holy Roman Empire and directed him to rule the vast, treeless steppes of southern Ukraine and annex the Black Sea peninsula of Crimea (see also *cardigan*). History gets a little murky at this point, depending on who is doing the telling, but Potemkin's detractors claim that when Catherine and several foreign dignitaries visited the barren flatlands under his control, Potemkin built entirely fake settlements with glowing fires and mobile herds of animals to make the desolate prairies look more inhabited. What is probably more likely is either that Catherine was party to the ruse (hoping to impress her entourage) or that Potemkin did little more than encourage his denizens to bring some spit and polish to their rural outpost.

Unfortunately, as is the case with many negative eponyms, whether or not the story is true is less important than the fact that it is how most of history remembers Potemkin. Fairly or not, today his name is invoked politically to represent what is believed to be a superficial cover-up of any undesirable truth, applied to everything from the Olympic Village constructed in Beijing in 2008 back to the concentration camps where the Nazis allowed visits during World War II.

Still, despite his notorious namesake, his alleged

venereal disease, and the undisputed fact that he lost his marbles near the end of his life, it is safe to say that Potemkin has fared better historically than Catherine the Great. Despite overwhelming and incontrovertible evidence to the contrary, many still claim she died after failed fornication with a horse.

⊲[gerrymander]⊳

v. to divide (a voting area) in such a way as to give an unfair advantage to one political party

—*Webster's New Universal Unabridged Dictionary,*
Second Edition

Were it not for the artistic pen of a political cartoonist, the sharp wit of a newspaper editor, and his own brazen corruption, Elbridge Gerry might be remembered for signing the Declaration of Independence and the Articles of Confederation and serving as both a governor and vice president of the United States. Instead, his legacy is an eternal pairing with a salamander.

Gerry was a lifelong Massachusetts man. Born in 1744 in Marblehead, he graduated from Harvard and served as a delegate from the Bay State (then the Bay Colony) to the Continental Congress in 1776, where he refused to sign the Constitution until it included a Bill of Rights. After a short stint in Congress, Gerry eventually joined the Democratic-Republican Party in

1800 and lost four consecutive bids to be the governor of Massachusetts before finally securing one-year terms in 1811 and 1812. He then blew his chance at a respectable legacy with some cartographical chicanery.

As the incumbent political party, Gerry's Democratic-Republicans hoped to preserve their power by redrawing several voting districts to concentrate opposing Federalist support in a few isolated districts while maintaining their own majority everywhere else. Benjamin Russell—the outraged editor of the *Centinel*, a Federalist newspaper—allegedly hung a map in his office illustrating the absurd new serpentine senatorial district of Essex County approved by then governor Gerry. Some early accounts report that celebrated portraitist Gilbert Stuart (who drew George Washington's face on the one-dollar bill) added a head, wings, and claws to the map to create the political "salamander" that Russell dubbed the "Gerry-mander." However, the more widely accepted theory is that painter, designer, and engraver Elkanah Tisdale drew the political cartoon of the now infamous namesake that would ultimately be published in the *Boston Gazette* and spawn a household word within months.

Most often employed by an incumbent power, gerrymandering typically either concentrates blocks of voters into one district to minimize their impact on other districts or spreads them out over multiple districts to dilute their power. Though a single word for it did not enter the political lexicon until after the Massachusetts map scandal of 1812, the practice had been around since the country's founding and exists to this day. In 1778, Patrick "Give Me Liberty or Give Me

Death" Henry and his anti-Federalist cronies famously overhauled a Virginia congressional district to keep future president James Madison out of the House of Representatives, while more than 220 years later Pennsylvania Republicans gerrymandered a finger-shaped district so meticulously that it stopped at a rival candidate's street and included his house but not his parking space.

As for the original gerrymanderer, the stinging portmanteau did little to ruin the Massachusetts governor's political career. The year after his namesake was coined, Gerry was chosen to be the fifth vice president of the United States, under James Madison, serving for a year and a half before dying of heart failure in 1814.

⊲❙ Houstonize ❙⊳

v. to beat up a Congressman
—*William Craigie's Dictionary of American English, 1940*
(reference courtesy of Jeffrey Kacirk's Forgotten English)

Though this word does not appear in most modern dictionaries, the story is simply too perfect to be lost to etymological history. Thankfully, Jeffrey Kacirk's *Forgotten English* rescued it from obscurity. Usage lasted for about one hundred years after Sam Houston delivered a bicameral beating to Representative William Stanbery in 1832.

Samuel Houston was a hard-drinking, straight-shooting pioneer renegade, who was born in the Shenandoah Valley of Virginia in 1793 and later ran away to live with a Cherokee tribe after his family moved to Tennessee. When he finally returned home in 1812, he built Tennessee's first schoolhouse; joined the army to fight the British in the War of 1812; and took an arrow in the leg and a bullet in the shoulder before leaving the military, becoming a lawyer, and being elected to the House of Representatives in 1822.

Houston eventually married and became the governor of Tennessee in 1827 but failed to serve even a single term before leaving his wife, becoming a drunk, and returning to live with the Cherokee Nation. He bigamously married a Cherokee widow and spent the next several years petitioning Washington to improve the plight of his adoptive tribe. Houston's noble cause and his notorious temper entered the national spotlight when he decided to beat the buckeyes out of Ohio congressman William Stanbery in 1832.

It all started with a contract to provide rations to the Native Americans who were about to take a long and unpleasant walk along the Trail of Tears thanks to President Andrew Jackson's Indian Removal Act of 1830. Houston, a friend of Jackson's but not always of his policies, was one of the bidders on the contract, and Stanbery decided to attack him verbally on the floor of the House of Representatives to indirectly incense Jackson, his political enemy. Full of piss and vinegar (and, likely, whiskey), Houston waited for Stanbery on

Pennsylvania Avenue, pummeled him mercilessly with a stick in broad daylight, and later pleaded not guilty to the assault, claiming he had acted in "self-defense."

The whole affair was a veritable cavalcade of American frontier folklore. Davy "Killed Him a Bear When He Was Only Three" Crockett had joined Houston in his opposition to Andrew "Old Hickory" Jackson's treatment of Native Americans. Meanwhile, Francis Scott "Star-Spangled Banner" Key was Houston's lawyer, and future president James "Napoleon of the Stump" Polk helped reduce his sentence after he was found guilty. After also losing a separate civil suit and being fined $500, Houston did what any sensible convict would do and fled to the then Mexican state of Texas.

Houston had an equally extraordinary second life in Texas. He was its first and only president when it became an independent republic in 1836, its senator after it joined the Union, and its governor until it tried to secede before the Civil War (which he opposed). Houston finally died of pneumonia in 1863, and despite *Houstonize* not surviving into modern times, this frontier maverick is remembered through his namesake city; countless streets, parks, and schools; and a slightly larger-than-life sixty-seven-foot statue in Huntsville, Texas.

⋞Haussmannize⋟

v. to open out, widen, and straighten streets, and generally rebuild, after the fashion in which Haussmann rebuilt Paris

—*Oxford English Dictionary*

While this word might not sound immediately pejorative, what is hidden in its generality is the fact that while Georges-Eugène Haussmann certainly inaugurated a newer, cleaner, and healthier nineteenth-century Paris, he also destroyed much of the medieval city, displaced thousands of low-income tenants, and incurred a public debt of hundreds of millions of francs, ultimately leading to his dismissal.

Haussmann was born in Paris in 1809 and studied law and music before entering civil service in France in his twenties and ultimately being appointed prefect of the Seine by Napoleon III (nephew of the Little Corporal and the last monarch of France) in 1853 to modernize the City of Light. By most historical accounts, much of Paris was a stinking, stagnant, and unsanitary mess through the first half of the nineteenth century. Haussmann overhauled all of that and converted the ancient serpentine streets into broad avenues and boulevards stretching out from a grand crossing in the center of the city. From Napoleon's view, this had the dual benefit of relieving congestion and inhibiting the ability of rioters to barricade narrow streets—a fact not lost on the social critics of the time.

Beyond the wide new thoroughfares, Baron Haussmann (he had assumed the courtesy title when he became a French senator in 1857) tore down apartment buildings and created open and airy greenways and gardens—shunting the underclass into the suburbs. He laid out the Bois de Boulogne park and built the Grand Opera House. He established a new water supply and sewer system and built new bridges and railway stations. And yes, the bourgeois were happy—until they received the bill.

Baron Haussmann turned out to be an endless faucet for public funds. After the initial investment, his works forced France to seek a loan of 250 million francs in 1865 and another 260 million four years later. More than fifteen years after he had begun his French face-lift—which overhauled more than half of the buildings in Paris and cost the state coffers more than 2 *billion* francs—Haussmann was finally fired in 1870. However, he was not forgotten. Urban developers around the world based dozens of cities on his redesign, including Moscow, Vienna, London, and Chicago, all emulating his razing of affordable housing to make way for an influx of wealth and beauty.

Haussmann died and was buried in Paris in 1891 and immortalized there through the Boulevard Haussmann; however, his name will always be fraught with contradiction. Despite inspiring the City Beautiful movement in the United States after his death, he remains, for many, the great-grandfather of gentrification and a potent symbol of unaffordable and socially irresponsible civic improvement.

Three years before he was fired, Haussmann was asked about why he felt he was chosen to oversee Paris's revitalization. He allegedly responded, "My qualifications? I was chosen as a demolition artist."

❧ boycott ❧

n. withdrawal from social or commercial interaction or cooperation with a group, nation, person, etc., intended as a protest or punishment

— Oxford English Dictionary

Historical relations between England and Ireland have always been strained, and Captain Charles Cunningham Boycott certainly did nothing to help matters. His unwillingness to negotiate resulted in his name being eternally maligned in more than a half dozen languages around the world.

The Emerald Isle has had a rough go of it over the years. St. Patrick and the Christians overwhelmed the pagan tribes in the fifth century AD, the Vikings wreaked havoc for a century or so, and then the Normans and the English settled in for the long haul. As the Irish Catholic landowners slowly lost their property to Protestant British settlers in the sixteenth and seventeenth centuries, times got pretty tough for your average Irish farmer.

Following the Act of Union (which was not nearly

as sexy as it sounds) between the Kingdom of Great Britain and the Kingdom of Ireland in 1801, absentee British landlords were common across the Irish isle, with local farmers renting and working the land. One of these landowners was John Crichton, the third earl of Erne, who hired Captain Charles Cunningham Boycott to manage his estates at Lough Mask House in Connaught, County Mayo, Ireland.

Born in Norfolk in 1832, Boycott served in the military before becoming a land agent in 1872. He had unfortunate historical timing for beginning this unsavory career (an 1843 Royal Commission described land-agent "middlemen" as "the most oppressive species of tyrant that ever lent assistance to the destruction of a country"). Boycott's new position came a short twenty years after the end of the Great Famine in Ireland (in which tenant farmers surviving solely on a diet of potatoes died by the hundreds of thousands) and just prior to the formation of the reformist Irish National Land League.

The Land League sought to protect farmers from exploitation through the "Three Fs" of fair rent, fixity of tenure, and free sale. When his tenants requested more reasonable rents in 1880 after several bad harvests, Boycott unwisely suggested a graphic fourth "F" for them to go and act upon themselves and even tried to evict one of them. The Land League's president, Charles Stewart Parnell, urged a local audience, "When a man takes a farm from which another had been evicted you must shun him on the roadside . . . , you must shun him in the streets . . . , you must shun him in the shop . . . by isolating him from the rest of his country as if he were the leper of old, you must show your detestation of the crime he has committed."

Boycott's workers left him, neighbors ignored him, his farm was vandalized, local stores would not serve him, and even the mailman would not deliver to him. Local officials organized a "Boycott Relief Expedition" under military protection to help save his harvest, but the land agent and his family were eventually forced to flee. Local newspapers began referring to successful ostracizing as "boycotting," and a lamentable legacy was born.

Boycott endured seventeen years of etymological smearing before dying back at home in England in 1897.

McCarthyism

n. a mid-20th century political attitude character-ized chiefly by opposition to elements held to be sub-versive and by the use of tactics involving personal attacks on individuals by means of widely publi-cized indiscriminate allegations esp. on the basis of unsubstantiated charges

—*Merriam-Webster's Collegiate Dictionary, Eleventh Edition*

The word still used today to chastise demagoguery and bullying political douchebaggery is the namesake of Joseph Raymond McCarthy, voted "the worst U.S.

senator" by the Senate press corps even *before* making his famous unsubstantiated claim in 1950 that he had an extensive list of known Communists working in the State Department.

The early years of the Cold War in the United States were fraught with anxiety over Commie infiltration, and the government conducted more than one hundred investigations in the early 1950s trying to root out the Red Threat. Born in 1908, "Tail-Gunner Joe" McCarthy was a marine combat pilot in World War II before becoming a senator in the 1940s and building his political reputation making unsubstantiated accusations of espionage and treason, leading to the imprisonment of hundreds of Americans and the unemployment of thousands. His namesake was first coined in a political cartoon in 1950 when Herblock (Herbert Lawrence Block) famously drew four Republicans trying to force a party elephant to balance atop a swaying stack of tar buckets, the largest one, on the top, labeled "McCarthyism."

While he is often associated with the sexier witch hunts of the *House* Un-American Activities Committee, McCarthy never browbeat any starlets or blacklisted any directors. As head of the *Senate* Permanent Subcommittee on Investigations, McCarthy was his own jackanapes and focused on Communist infiltration of the State Department, government broadcasters, overseas librarians (whose card catalogs were allegedly bursting with burnable communist propaganda), and the U.S. Army. However, his name has since come to represent the entire era of paranoia and persecution.

McCarthy was ultimately unable to prove any

wrongdoing by anyone anywhere, and his attacks on the army for alleged security lapses were followed the next year by separate and unrelated charges of abuse of power brought *against* him by the army (it is the thirty-six days of televised proceedings of *these* hearings that people most remember). He was ultimately acquitted, but the damage to his reputation was done. McCarthy's fellow senators ultimately censured him in 1954 through a decisive dressing-down vote of 67–22, and he lost all of his political power, leading President Eisenhower to refer to his former nemesis's legacy as "McCarthywasm." The senator slipped increasingly into bouts of alcoholism and finally died from inflammation of his liver in 1957 at the tender age of forty-eight.

During his life, McCarthy had fully embraced his namesake, even co-opting it for the title of his book: *McCarthyism: The Fight for America*. But cartoonist Herblock ultimately had the last laugh regarding his creation. He insisted there was "nothing particularly ingenious about the term, which is simply used to represent a national affliction that can hardly be described in any other way. If anyone has a prior claim on it, he's welcome to the word and to the junior senator from Wisconsin along with it. I will also throw in a set of free dishes and a case of soap."

CHAPTER EIGHT

Culture & Commerce

⊰[mausoleum]⊱

n. any tomb of more than ordinary splendor, especially a tomb designed for the members of a great or
royal family; humorously applied to any large building or room regarded as like such a tomb

—*Webster's New Universal Unabridged Dictionary,*
Second Edition

If you have ever wondered whether size matters to
women, look no further than Queen Artemisia of
Caria. When her husband, King Mausolus, died in 353
BC, she ordered a tomb to be built for him that would
become one of the Seven Wonders of the Ancient
World. Though the monument is long gone, the king's
legacy remains through his name association with any
preposterously oversized coffin-holder.

Mausolus and Artemisia lived in Halicarnassus in

what is now southwest Turkey. Together, they ruled for twenty-four years and spent a fortune in tax funds to make their capital a spectacular fortress with paved streets, a Greek-style theater, and statues and buildings in brilliant marble. When Mausolus died, Artemisia was so stricken with grief that she drank a portion of his ashes daily for three years before finally dying of a broken heart. Between cremation cocktails and before her swan song, Artemisia also managed to hire the finest Greek architects and sculptors to create a staggering sepulchral monument to her husband, which would not be finished until after her death in 350 BC. The palatial tomb itself towered well higher than one hundred feet on a base nearly the size of a football field, and all four sides featured statues and bas-relief carvings of Mausolus and his queen, gods and goddesses, centaurs and warriors, and Greeks and Amazons. Mounted stone warriors stood guard over the tomb, while stone lions flanked the stairs. Finally, atop the tomb's massive pyramidal roof rode four enormous stone horses pulling a great bronze chariot.

Along with the Great Pyramid of Giza, the Hanging Gardens of Babylon, the Colossus of Rhodes, the Lighthouse of Alexandria, the Statue of Zeus at Olympia, and the Temple of Artemis at Ephesus, what the Greeks would eventually call *Mausoleion* (in honor of the dead king) became one of the Seven Wonders of the Ancient World. It survived Alexander III, pirate attacks, and nearly 1,800 years of wear and tear—but not the hand of Poseidon, Greek god of earthquakes. After finally crumbling in 1375, its scattered stones were used by the Crusaders to fortify Bodrum Castle in the late fifteenth century. Grave robbers stole much of the riches of the central chamber in the sixteenth century, and the British graciously "preserved" the rest in the nineteenth. A statue of Mausolus resides in the British Museum today.

Groucho Marx's famous gimme question "Who is buried in Grant's Tomb?" refers to the New York City landmark that is the largest mausoleum in North America. Like Mausolus, General Grant was entombed with his wife, Julia, who did not drink a daily dose of his ashes or commission his ostentatious resting place but did state lovingly in her memoirs that "the light of his glorious fame still reaches out to me, falls upon me, and warms me."

⊰ ottoman ⊱

n. a low, cushioned seat without a back or arms
—*Webster's New Universal Unabridged Dictionary,*
Second Edition

It is truly a shame that a man once seated at a throne atop the entire world should be reduced to a lowly stuffed footstool, but such is the unfortunate legacy of Osman I.

In the late thirteenth century, a shift in the balance of world power was taking place. Following the death

of Genghis Khan, hordes of Mongols were pillaging
their way west toward Europe at the same time that the
Christian Byzantine Empire began losing its stronghold
over mostly Muslim Asia Minor. From the middle of
this cultural sandwich rose the Ottoman Empire, which
would rule for more than six hundred years.

Born in 1259, Osman I was the sultan of Anatolia
(modern-day Turkey) in the early fourteenth century.
He managed to band his Turkish countrymen together
with the mercenaries and refugees fleeing the Mongo-
lian raiders and successfully established his people as
the Islamic successors to the Byzantine Empire (the
eastern version of the Holy Roman one next door).
Building on this legacy, within two hundred years
the Ottoman Empire sprawled across most of western Asia, southeastern Europe, and northern Africa.
Its capital, Constantinople, was the crossroads for the
Eastern and Western worlds for most of the prior mil-
lennium. Osman himself was celebrated in poem and
song for centuries after for his bravery, his beauty, and,
strangely, his "wondrous length and strength of arm."
Turkish delight on a moonlit night, indeed.

How Osman became a glorified hassock is a bit
more of a mystery. The *Oxford English Dictionary* places
the first written usage of *ottoman* as furniture in 1789,
from no less than jaunty trendsetter Thomas Jeffer-
son. Europeans in the eighteenth century simply could
not get enough of the marvels of the Near East and
provided an eager market for the pillows, carpets, and
low-slung furnishings that satisfied the fantasies of an
exotic Arabian night. The rich textiles imported from

the Ottoman Empire were variously called *ottomane* (French), *ottomana* (Italian), *otomana* (Spanish), and *Ottomane* (German). Following the lead of the French, the English word morphed from the textured fabrics to divans and then from chairs to footstools.

Osman died in 1326, but the Ottoman Empire was not dissolved and succeeded by the Republic of Turkey until 1923. Despite his namesake being well represented as a home furnishing by that point, Osman and the Turkish wards of his empire did ultimately have their etymological revenge against the Western infidels. Though it had been called Byzantium, New Rome, and Stamboul at various points in history, in 1930 Constantinople was officially renamed Istanbul— the Turkish name for the city since the tenth century. The Four Lads immortalized the cartographical coup in their swing hit "Istanbul (Not Constantinople)" in 1953, as did a revival of the song in 1990 by alt-pop darlings They Might Be Giants.

◅| nicotine |▻

n. a poisonous alkaloid, $C_{10}H_{14}N_2$, found in tobacco leaves, from which it is extracted as a colorless, oily, acrid, transparent liquid and used, ordinarily in an aqueous solution of its sulfate, as an insecticide

—*Webster's New Universal Unabridged Dictionary,*
Second Edition

While other Frenchmen have since been described as colorless, oily, acrid, and transparent, nicotine's namesake was also a diplomat and a scholar.

Ah, young love. In 1559 in Portugal, the regents for fresh-faced six-year-old French princess Marguerite de Valois and strapping five-year-old King Sebastian of Portugal discussed a pre-prepubescent love connection between these two naifs. Jean Nicot de Villemain was the French ambassador to Portugal in charge of negotiations. Though the royal union was ultimately unsuccessful, Nicot did manage to kindle France's love affair with smoking. He sent back tobacco.

Native Americans had been smoking *tabaco* ritualistically for literally thousands of years before Christopher Columbus and crew were introduced to it by the islanders of Hispaniola. On Columbus's second voyage to the New World, a tribe of Haitians demonstrated the sniffing of dried tobacco leaves as snuff. Though it is believed that French monk and explorer André Thévet may have been the first person to introduce the tobacco plant to Europe in the early sixteenth century, it was Nicot who garnered fame after sending plants and seeds to the French court. It was snuff, in particular, that turned queen mother Catherine de' Medici's head. She used it medicinally to treat her son's migraines, and the Parisian elite could soon not get enough of this new wonder drug. Part of the often poisonous nightshade family, by the late 1500s all tobacco plants fell under the genus *Nicotiana*, in honor of the French diplomat.

It took more than two hundred years for nicotine

itself to be isolated by chemists as a poison in 1828, and there was an early forensic case in 1851 in which Belgian count Bocarmé was found guilty of murdering his brother-in-law with tobacco leaf extract. Created from dried tobacco leaves, a typical cigarette contains approximately one milligram of Nicot's legacy as a stimulant, which is believed to be largely responsible for smoking's addictiveness. In addition to its appearance in cigars, cigarettes, and pipes, nicotine was widely used as an insecticide into the twentieth century. Outside of recreational and pest-control use, tobacco leaves are also used to induce vomiting in Brazil, to prevent baldness in Colombia, to ease painful menstruation in Cuba, to treat snake bites in Ecuador, to repel insects in Iran, and to induce labor in Tanzania.

It is impossible to estimate how many lives Jean Nicot de Villemain has touched over the centuries, whether in leaf, gum, or even patch form. Despite being a true intellectual and the creator of one of the very first French dictionaries (published posthumously in 1606), it is the addictive weed for which he will always be remembered. His (perhaps self-promoting) dictionary defined *nicotiane* as "an herb of marvelous virtue against all wounds, ulcers, lupis, or other eroding ulcers of the face, herpes, and other such things." He died in 1600 at the age of seventy.

⊰ pinchbeck ⊱

n. a thing that is false, counterfeit, cheap, or worthless; spec. something that appears valuable but is
actually cheap or tawdry; also: the state or condition of being tawdry or worthless

— *Oxford English Dictionary*

The word *pinchbeck* comes from the name of Christopher Pinchbeck, a master craftsman and inventor of
an inexpensive imitation-gold alloy in the eighteenth
century. Today this talented artist joins the lowly
ranks of those whose names have been reduced to
junk, including St. Audrey (see *tawdry*) and the entire
city of Birmingham, England, from which we get the
word *brummagem*, meaning "cheaply showy," based on
the counterfeit coins produced there in the seventeenth
century.

Pinchbeck was a watch- and toymaker with a small
shop on Fleet Street in London. Born in 1670, he is
immortalized by the unique alloy he introduced in 1732,
the year of his death. All gold alloys (and brass) employ
some combination of zinc and copper. However, while
most of his predecessors used up to two-thirds zinc,
Pinchbeck struck upon a novel ratio of 15 percent zinc
to 85 percent copper that rendered his product superlative. Beyond the color, which was indistinguishable
from gold, was the staying power of the glow. Pinchbeck's imitation-gold toys, snuffboxes, sword hilts, and
watches made him an overnight sensation among those

without the means to buy the genuine article. And yet they were by no means reserved for chimney sweeps and chambermaids.

The 1700s were a pretty rough time to be a well-heeled traveler through the English countryside. More bothersome than the natural inconvenience of single-digit horsepower transportation were the thieves and highwaymen who waylaid travelers. It became customary among the upper class, when traveling unguarded, to carry pinchbeck ornamentations both to reduce their losses in a robbery and to discourage would-be "gentlemen of the road," who conspired with the innkeepers and carriage drivers sending out alerts when a wealthy customer was on the move.

So popular became the watchmaker's creations among the lords and ladies that within two years of Pinchbeck's death, Henry Fielding noted in his 1734 comic play *The Intriguing Chambermaid* that "the Nobility and Gentry run so much into Pinchbeck, that he had not dispos'd of two Gold Watches this Month." Needless to say, this popularity caught the attention of true goldworkers, who brought legal proceedings against poor Pinchbeck and succeeded in limiting his creations to shoe buckles, buttons, and the like to avoid what they regarded as unfair competition.

Unfortunately, Pinchbeck's golden era was short-lived. His trade secret for the manufacture of his alloy, and his great artistry, died with him in 1732. The compromising work of his successors and the eventual introduction of gold electroplating, all still described as pinchbeck, eventually degraded the once proud name to represent any false, counterfeit, or cheap imitation—a regrettable legacy for a master craftsman.

⊲Listerine⊳

n. an antiseptic solution

—Oxford English Dictionary

Single women the world over rightfully curse the men who popularized the phrase *often a bridesmaid but never a bride*, many not realizing that it was part of a wildly successful advertising campaign for Listerine in the 1920s that warned young ladies that their bad breath might leave them old maids before their "tragic" thirtieth birthday. Had he still been living, no one would have been cursing louder than eminent British surgeon Baron Joseph Lister, who spent the last years of his life desperately trying to dissociate himself from a product that he neither invented nor endorsed.

Hospital wards in the midnineteenth century were stinking, seeping cesspools of infection. Windows were generally kept closed (limiting the influx of fresh air), surgeons did not wash their instruments or their hands prior to procedures, and wounds were rarely, if ever, flushed clean, providing literal breeding grounds for deadly microorganisms. When Joseph Lister was a young surgeon in the Male Accident Ward of the Glasgow Royal Infirmary in the 1860s, more than half of his amputation patients died from sepsis, a bacterial wound infection.

Lister became fascinated with Louis Pasteur's emerging theories on rot and fermentation and was convinced that his findings could be applied to medicine. At the time, Britain was more concerned with the cleanliness of its sewers than its hospitals, and carbolic acid had been used for years to improve the odor of its municipal muck. In 1865 Lister decided that what was good enough for British sewage was good enough for British patients, and he began swabbing his surgical tools and his patients' wounds with carbolic acid. His patient mortality rate instantly dropped by 35 percent. He formalized his sterile operating procedures in 1867 (including forcing surgeons to wear clean gloves and wash their hands before and after surgeries), and they were quickly adopted worldwide.

Lister was made a baron in 1883 and enjoyed an extraordinarily successful medical career and respectable retirement until his death in 1912 at the age of eighty-four. For his pioneering efforts, he became the namesake of the Royal Society's prestigious Lister Medal and England's Lister Institute of Preventive Medicine. He was commemorated on two postal stamps in 1965 and has public monuments in both London and Glasgow. Unfortunately, it is the now ubiquitous Listerine that provides him with the most name recognition today.

In 1879, twelve years after Lister's groundbreaking discoveries, Dr. Joseph Lawrence and Jordan Wheat Lambert used Lister's research to formulate a surgical antiseptic that was eventually recommended for dentists in 1895. Over the shy and unassuming surgeon's objections, the Lambert Pharmacal Company marketed the product as Listerine and by 1914 was selling it as the first over-the-counter mouthwash. According to company legend, once the general manager heard that there was a medical term for bad breath (halitosis), his admen embarked on a spectacular 1920s campaign castigating the social disgrace of foul mouth odor and skyrocketing Lambert Pharmacal's profits into the millions.

Thankfully, for his sake, Lister did not live to witness the decades of absurd and misleading Listerine marketing ploys that hawked his namesake as everything from dandruff suppressant, deodorant, and sore throat remedy to gonorrhea treatment, aftershave, and floor cleaner.

ᵈ⟨ crapper ⟩ᵇ

n. toilet
—*Merriam-Webster's Collegiate Dictionary, Eleventh Edition*

Mention that you are reading a book on notorious eponyms and you will likely receive a yawn, a condescending eye roll, or an excited outburst that Sir Thomas Crapper invented the flush toilet. The first two responses demonstrate that there is just no accounting for some people's taste, while the third reflects the remarkable staying power of a satirical pseudobiography that launched one of the most ubiquitous urban legends in history. Let us make several things clear. Thomas Crapper most certainly did not invent the toilet, but it might be possible that we invoke his namesake when we ascend the porcelain throne.

Wallace Reyburn was a war correspondent, magazine editor, and humorist, who wrote a good many books in his life, some more serious (and factual) than others, but 1969's tongue-in-cheek *Flushed with Pride: The Story of Thomas Crapper* and 1971's teat-in-sling *Bust-up: The Uplifting Tale of Otto Titzling and the Development of the Bra* proved to be swallowed whole by a generous portion of their readership. Despite the rampant puns in the latter "bra-ography"—including an assistant named Hans Delving and a female athlete named Lois Lung—the completely fictional Titzling eventually became a supposedly real answer to a Trivial Pursuit question. Meanwhile, *Flushed* describes Crapper's good friend "B.S." and the "many dry runs" required to perfect the "Crapper W.C. Cistern." People have been spouting this satire as fact for the last forty years.

The truth is that Thomas P. Crapper did exist. He was a British plumber, born around 1836, who owned his own plumbing company and widely popularized flush toilets, but his connection to modern word usage is somewhat murkier. Certainly the word *crap*, derived from the Dutch *krappe*, precedes him by centuries, first appearing in English in 1440. Likewise, the prototypes and early patents for our modern flushing toilets are generally attributed to Sir John Harrington at the end of the sixteenth century and Alexander Cummings in the 1770s, decades before Crapper created his first movement. But Crapper's company in London did pioneer the use of the floating ballcock (to avoid overflow) and outfitted several royal lavatories, including those of Edward VII and George V. The resourceful Crapper was never knighted for his contributions, however, as is often alleged.

While fanciful anecdotes and jokes abound, it is still possible that our use of both *crapper* and *crap* are connected to the British plumber. *Crapper* first appears in the *Oxford English Dictionary* as a privy in 1932 in American usage, and *crap* is not used to mean defecation until 1937. One prevailing theory is that American soldiers serving in World War I traveled to Britain and spent a fair amount of time staring at "Thomas Crapper & Co. Ltd." fixtures while dropping personal bombs and brought Thomas's namesake back to the United States. *Crapper* thus slowly entered the lexicon over the next decade. Meanwhile, the name's close connection to the contents carried helped transform *crap* (a traditional word for chaff, residue, and rubbish) into its stinking incarnation today. Crapper himself retired from the crapper business in 1904 and is immortalized on a series of manhole covers in Westminster Abbey. He passed in 1910.

Yet while Crapper's offal association might be debatable (see also *fontange*), there is a solid quartet of historical heroes who share the dubious distinction of having their names (and, sometimes, faces) directly conjoined with voiding vessels. Because only *vespasienne* appears in modern usage (*Oxford English Dictionary*), all have been relegated to footnote status here:

vespasienne

In chronological order, our first stop on the Excrement Express is Italy. One year after Nero committed suicide in AD 68, the great military leader Titus Flavius Vespasianus (generally referred to as Vespasian) became Emperor of Rome. His primary goal seemed to be to institute new taxes, wherever possible, to fill the royal coffers and fund his grand new ventures—including construction of the immense Colosseum, which would not be completed until his son's rule. One of his most creative moneymaking schemes was a "urine tax" imposed on public facilities. To maximize his supply-chain loop, he sold the collected urine to launderers, who aged it in giant vats (until it converted to ammonia) and then used it for bleaching. Italians henceforth called urinals *vespianos*, leading to the French *vespasiennes*, which was then absorbed into English. Vespasian was relieved of his mortal strain in AD 79 when he died of a diarrhea-racked fever.

Oliver's skull

Roughly 1,500 years later in England, a civil war over haircuts and political succession was under way. The short-haired, Parliament-supporting Roundheads were facing up against the curly tresses of the monarch-loving Royalists. The Roundheads ultimately won a victory in 1651 that would eventually establish a parliamentary monarchy 150 years later, but short-term leadership of the country fell to the alternately revered and reviled Oliver Cromwell. While soothing their wounds from their military losses over a few pints, the Royalists drunkenly stumbled across the hilarious notion of dubbing their chamber pots "Oliver's skulls." The slang stuck well into the 1800s. Cromwell himself died in 1658 (somewhat ironically) from a urinary tract infection. Three years later, after the Royalists had returned to power, his buried body was exhumed, hanged at Tyburn (see *derrick*), thrown in a pit, and then beheaded. There is no historical record to confirm whether his skull was subsequently retrieved and repurposed.

sacheverell

Political tensions were not much relieved in the decades that followed, and soon the divine-right-of-kings-supporting Tories and the crown-threatening Whigs were at each other's throats. In 1709, ardent Tory and clergyman Dr. Henry Sacheverell successfully pissed off the entire Whig party in a series of sermons that accused the Whigs of being too tolerant of religious dissenters. His fomenting language initially led to his short suspension from preaching and an entry in the *Oxford English Dictionary* as a synonym for a stove blower, the implication being that he was famous for "blowing the coals of dissension." However, more germane to the topic here, his name also became synonymous with chamber pots after several resourceful Whigs managed to manufacture the common household items with a portrait of Dr. Sacheverell painted on the bottom.

twiss

The Irish thought this piss-pot portraiture hilarious but had no appropriate target for their streams for nearly seventy years until British travel writer Richard Twiss published his decidedly unflattering *Tour in Ireland* in 1775. It was an enormous bestseller in his home country of England but struck heavy ire in the land to the west by asserting that the Irish primarily consumed whiskey and were notable for little more than the thickness of their legs—particularly the women. In response, a Dublin pottery company began selling a chamber pot called a "twiss" that included a portrait of its namesake, facing forward with an open mouth. Accounts (and, perhaps, versions) of its caption vary, but the general gist is as follows:

> *Here you may behold a liar,*
> *Well deserving of hell-fire:*
> *Every one who likes may piss*
> *Upon the learned Doctor Twiss.*

As an editorial footnote to these etymological footnotes, any reader now inspired to sully the most extraordinarily large urinals east of the Mississippi River needs only swing open the saloon doors of the Old Town Bar in New York City, home to the grand porcelain towers of the Hinsdale Company, whose magnificence dwarf even the mightiest sword. In contrast, the Old Town's crappers are nothing to speak of.

❦ Rube Goldberg ❧

adj. accomplishing by complex means what seemingly could be done simply
—*Merriam-Webster's Collegiate Dictionary, Eleventh Edition*

Though once revered and beloved as a comic icon, Rube Goldberg's name has recently taken a pejorative turn and come to represent overcomplication and waste—a true shame for this superlative and Pulitzer Prize–winning artist.

Reuben Garret Lucius Goldberg was born in 1883 and longed for the life of an artist. His father longed otherwise, and Goldberg earned an engineering degree from UC Berkeley in 1904 before designing sewer systems for the city of San Francisco. Goldberg quickly had his fill of municipal misery and captured a gofer job in the sports department of the *San Francisco Chronicle.* His constant doodling caught the eye of the editor and eventually earned him a promotion and then a ticket to New York as a full-time cartoonist. He was fully syndicated by 1915.

Goldberg created silly characters such as Boob McNutt, Lala Palooza, and Mike and Ike ("they look alike"), as well as numerous series of purely entertainment fare in the 1920s and 1930s. Like Theodor "Dr. Seuss" Geisel, Goldberg turned his talent toward political cartoons during World War II. These would earn him a Pulitzer Prize in 1948 but would also drive him to change the last names of his sons after he began receiving threatening hate mail.

But it was Goldberg's creation of Professor Lucifer Gorgonzola Butts and his wacky inventions that would cement his legacy and earn him a retrospective at the Smithsonian Institution in Washington, DC, near the end of his life. The professor's inventions featured impossibly complicated chain reactions (often involving animals) to perform startlingly mundane tasks. A classic example was his "simplified pencil-sharpener" that required moths to eat a flannel shirt—to drop a shoe—to step on a switch to heat an electric iron—to burn a hole in some pants—to create the smoke that would chase an opossum from a tree and into a basket—to pull a rope and lift a cage—to release a woodpecker to chew on a pencil to sharpen it.

The drawings were wildly popular and spawned children's board and video games as well as emulation in countless feature films, animations, sitcoms, commercials, and science shows. They inspired an annual competition at Purdue University in which winning entries must use as many mechanical steps as possible to perform a simple task, such as dispensing hand sanitizer, juicing an orange, or making a hamburger. Unfortunately, they have also been used by political pundits and even actual journalists as an insult, by describing everything from complicated health-care bills and Social Security to campaign-finance reform and military withdrawals as Rube Goldberg designs.

Goldberg retired in 1964 to become a sculptor and died in 1970 at the age of eighty-seven. He was posthumously commemorated on a postage stamp featuring his work and had an award named for him by the National Cartoonists Society. However, despite his mass appeal and extraordinary success, Goldberg was clearly a bit of a social skeptic. He once noted acerbically that his inventions were a "symbol of man's capacity for exerting maximum effort to achieve minimal results."

·CHAPTER NINE·

Style & Fashion

◁[tawdry]▷

adj. of the nature of cheap finery; showy or gaudy without real value

—*Oxford English Dictionary*

Our modern usage of the word *tawdry* comes from a slurring of the name of St. Audrey, a young woman who regretted wearing pretty things but not maintaining her virginity.

Some virgins hold up better than others over the course of history. Poor Aethelthryth was an Anglo-Saxon princess born around AD 640 to the King of East Anglia, the area around Suffolk, England. Her name, and her reputation, certainly took a beating during the Norman years that followed, as her name was changed first to Etheldreda and then further to Audrey.

Audrey was a sweet kid who loved to wear gold

chains and necklaces. As was expected of her, she married, only to be widowed three years later. The Anglo-Saxon scuttlebutt at the time was that she had taken a perpetual vow of virginity and that her first marriage was never consummated. Poor Audrey became a nun for a time but eventually married again, dutifully bowing to political and familial pressures. Her new young husband did not share her piety and continually tried to pick the locks of the royal chastity belt. He even went so far as to try to bribe their local bishop, St. Wilfrid of York, to free his wife from her virginal commitment. But the bishop appreciated her moxie and helped Audrey flee south to Ely, in the English county of Cambridgeshire, with her husband close on her heels.

Ecclesiastical legend has it that God himself rescued Audrey from an amorous fate by raising the tide for seven days around the promontory she had climbed to escape her mate. This cold shower finally sent her husband into the arms of someone more accommodating and freed up Audrey to dedicate herself completely to the church, becoming the abbess of Ely. She finally died at around forty years old with a bulging tumor on her neck, which she believed God had inflicted on her for the necklaces she wore in her younger days.

Audrey was eventually canonized and became the patron saint of Cambridge University, neck and throat ailments, and widows. In the years following her sainthood, the Isle of Ely would hold an annual fair every June 23—the feast day of St. Audrey—at which merchants would sell gold necklaces and, particularly, lace scarves called "St. Audrey's lace." Over time, these fineries became cheap trinkets hawked to the county wenches as "S'nt-Audrey lace" and, finally, *tawdry* lace.

Even as early as 1579, Edmund Spenser referenced poor Audrey in *The Shepheardes Calender*: "Binde your fillets faste, And gird in your waste, For more finesse, with a tawdrie lace."

By the eighteenth century, the word *tawdry* had come to represent anything gaudy, cheap, or tasteless—a poor legacy for yet another innocent virgin of history (see *Catherine wheel*).

⊲|lavaliere|⊳

n. a pendant on a fine chain that is worn as a necklace

⊲|lavalier microphone|⊳

n. a small microphone hung around the neck of the user

—*Merriam-Webster's Collegiate Dictionary, Eleventh Edition*

What can be said of a woman who endured a tumultuous social roller-coaster ride from naïve jailbait distraction to merry monarch mistress to hair-shirted convent crasher? She had an elegant neck, liked pretty things, and now has a nearly obsolete piece of amplification equipment named for her.

King Louis XIV of France had the longest reign of any monarch in European history. For more than seventy-two years, between 1643 and 1715, the Sun King centralized his government, reformed his military (see *martinet*), and expanded his monarchy into new colonies across the ocean. To let off some royal steam, Louis indulged his love for French ladies and, in addition to his two wives, appointed (it was a semi-official court position) multiple *maîtresses-en-titre* (chief mistresses) during his extraordinarily long monarchy (see also *fontange*).

In 1661, the lovely princess Henrietta Anne of England moved in at King Louis' court at Fontainebleu. Though she was the new wife of his brother, the strangely intimate relationship between her and Louis raised a few eyebrows and prompted Henrietta to seek out other distractions for the king, to quell suspicions. They had not looked far when Louis' eyes fell on Henrietta's seventeen-year-old maid of honor—Louise Françoise de La Baume Le Blanc. She was a blond-haired, blue-eyed beauty who came to adore the king as their relationship blossomed in short order from a scandal-avoiding smoke screen to a true romance. Unfortunately, her religious upbringing ultimately tortured her conscience and, within a year, she fled to a convent to escape the royal affair. Louis ultimately convinced her to return, and the two embarked on a semisecretive reproductive spree that would result in at least six children, only two of whom survived.

By 1667, the king had cooled a bit on Louise and again set his sights on a younger paramour. As a parting gift from his bedchamber, the king made Louise Duchess de La Vallière and Duchess de Vaujours. By this time, the newly dubbed duchess was already a glamorous fashion plate across Europe and had introduced a number of stylish accoutrements to the populace, including a jeweled pendant worn on a chain around the neck, soon dubbed the *lavallièr.*

Unfortunately, shiny jewels were not enough to help Louise stomach her new social role. The king's new mistress was married, and Louise was once again used as a diversion to redirect attention away from an adulterous relationship. In an eye-popping display of religious hypocrisy, she even became the godmother of the mistress's first daughter with the king. The spiritual stress was too great for the pious Louise, and she began donning the torturous shirt of coarse animal hair typically reserved for self-flagellating penitents. Louis finally allowed her to enter a convent in 1674, and she lived there as Sister Louise of Mercy until her death in 1710.

Worn around the neck, the lavalier microphone became popular in the 1960s but has since been replaced by newer, more attractive, cordless models, with the originals now collecting dust in countless church basements and convents. More recently, the Wakefield twins in the ever-popular *Sweet Valley High* book series were identifiable by the matching gold lavalieres they wore in every book—a fitting pop culture tribute to the seventeen-year-old French darling who started it all.

⊰|fontange|⊱

n. a knot of ribbons formerly worn as a headdress;
a commode

> —*Webster's New Universal Unabridged Dictionary,*
> *Second Edition*

Only a small cadre of famed temptresses can boast of
riding the French royal pony during the heyday of its
world dominance. Fewer still have been able to create a fashion sensation from an absurd outcropping of
human hair (see also *pompadour*). But only the Duchess de Fontanges also succeeded in having her sartorial
namesake once mistaken for a British toilet.

Just two years after King Louis XIV traded the
Duchess de La Vallière (see *lavaliere*) for a younger mistress, his eyes strayed again toward another fresh-faced
seventeen-year-old—Marie Angélique de Scorailles de
Roussille. Marie was a lady-in-waiting for his sister-
in-law, the two were soon lovers, and the red-haired
beauty was named the Duchess de Fontanges in the
south of France. Legend has it that one day, after losing
her cap during a hunt, she tied her hair back with ribbons and left a few curls to hang coquettishly across her
brow. This new coiffure *de fontange* tickled the king's
fancy and quickly became part of a fashion vanguard
across the kingdom.

Unfortunately, as with all fashion fads embraced during Louis XIV's reign, the simple ribbons of the original

fontange were quickly carried to absurd heights, resulting in a two-foot-tall mélange of human hair, feathers, bows, jewels, and gummy linen. Fontanges became so tall and complex that they became nearly impossible to wear, and the king allegedly tried to abolish them in 1699. Young Marie did not live long enough to see the grand heights to which her namesake ascended. One year after becoming a chief mistress, she delivered the king a stillborn child, was shipped off to a convent, and died shortly after, in 1681, at the age of twenty.

But her namesake lived on. Mary Howarth describes the fontange in her section of *Every Woman's Encyclopedia* from 1910: "It was a framework of cap wire about half a yard in height, divided into tiers and positively covered with bands of muslin, ribbons, flowers, chenille, and upstanding aigrettes. To each tier of the structure names were given such as the Duke, the duchess, the Capuchin, the Solitary One, the Asparagus, the Cabbage, the Cat, the Organ Pipe, the First or Second Sky, and the Mouse."

That "framework of cap wire" was known in England at the time as a "commode," and that became the British name for the fontange. However, tempting as it may be to believe that a few saucy Brits dubbed the French hairstyle a "commode" as an intentional insult, the history of usage simply does not play out. It took nearly two hundred more years for *commode* to morph from hairstyle to furniture to chamber pot. But do not despair. There are plenty of other instances of *noms pour les toilettes* (see *crapper*).

⊲ pompadour ⊳

n. a woman's hairdo in which the hair is swept up high from the forehead, usually over a roll

n. a man's hairdo in which the hair is brushed up straight from the forehead

—*Webster's New Universal Unabridged Dictionary,*
Second Edition

The somewhat absurd hairstyle beloved by French courtesans and Elvis impersonators alike is the namesake of Madame de Pompadour, former mistress of King Louis XV.

Madame de Pompadour was born Jeanne-Antoinette Poisson in Paris in 1721. By all accounts she was extraordinarily beautiful, intelligent, and well educated. She also had a bit of a stage mother who ensured that she would learn to play the clavichord, paint, get married, become friends with Voltaire, and charm the pantaloons off the king, all before her twenty-fourth birthday.

Within a month of their meeting, Louis XV had established Jeanne-Antoinette at Versailles as his mistress. He wooed her with an estate at Pompadour and gave her the title of marquise (more hoity than a countess, but not as toity as a duchess) so that she could appear in his court. Six months after seducing the king, the new Madame de Pompadour legally separated from her husband and began a lifelong crusade to have things named for her.

Despite being loathed by the upper crust for her bourgeois background, she became a trusted adviser to the king, a devoted patron of the decorative arts, and the unrivaled center of the Parisian fashion scene. Her support of porcelain manufacturing led to the creation of Pompadour pink, a specific color for fine ceramics. Handbags, silks embroidered with sprigs of flowers, and even richly plumed birds (*Xipholena punicea*, the pompadour cotinga) all bore her name. Though she was only his mistress for five years, legend has it that after she died at age forty-two from congested lungs, a grieving Louis XV commissioned his craftsmen to create the oblong marquise, or navette, cut for diamonds to remind him of the delicate shape of her mouth.

Well after her death, a purple-uniformed regiment of the British Army in the eighteenth and nineteenth centuries was nicknamed the Pompadours, owing either to purple being her favorite color or—depending on the discretion of your source—the color of her underwear. Urban legend has also suggested that the classic French champagne coupe may have been modeled from her breast—Marie Antoinette is another contender for this distinction—despite being designed several decades before either woman's bosom sprang into public consciousness.

But it was her hair that brought her infamy (see also *fontange*). Though she classically wore it in loose rolls around her face, the style that became associated with her name eventually involved sweeping the hair upward to hang high above the forehead. And it was not simply for the ladies. As early as 1885, no less than the *Atlanta*

Constitution newspaper recommended it for the gents: "The *pompadour* is the most convenient way possible to wear the hair. It is cool, and simply running your fingers through it when you get up dresses it for the day."

Elvis surely agreed.

⊲│ havelock │⊳

n. a white cloth covering for the cap, with a flap hanging over the neck, to be worn by soldiers as a protection from the sun's heat

— Oxford English Dictionary

Depending on one's age and geographical location, havelocks are reminders of either early French Foreign Legion films or amusement-park mullet protectors. Either way, they are the namesake of a gallant and evangelical British soldier—Sir Henry Havelock.

Havelock was born the son of a wealthy shipbuilder in what is now Sunderland, England, in 1795. He became a military man by the age of twenty, as did his three brothers, and served dutifully for more than three decades, primarily in India. He was a dedicated soldier and devout Baptist who distributed Bibles to his fellow soldiers and taught Bible-study classes. He fought valiantly in the Burmese and Afghan wars and, most famously, in the insurgent siege of Lucknow during the Indian Mutiny of 1857. It was there that he modified a type of helmet covering used since the Crusades to protect men from sunstroke when fighting in hot climates.

Dubbed "havelocks," they were quickly embraced by Union military brass in the American Civil War as well. The *New York Times* wrote in May 1861 that "British officers in India, and in the Crimea, furnished their soldiers with thick, white, linen cap covers, reflecting instead of absorbing the heat of the sun, and having a cape long enough to fully cover the back of the neck." Early in the war, there were "Ladies Havelock Associations" in more than one hundred towns and cities across the United States, furiously sewing more than 100,000 "Havelock Cap-covers" for Union troops marching across "the scorching plains of the South." Sadly, and unbeknownst to the well-intentioned seamstresses, many soldiers reported that the havelocks from home made them even more uncomfortable by thwarting air circulation around their necks. A number of soldiers cannibalized their cap covers to strain coffee or wash dishes, and others simply discarded them completely.

As for Havelock himself, he died of dysentery in 1857 following his agonizing heroism during the Lucknow siege by Sepoy rebels. He lived long enough to accept a baronetcy for his victories, but he died before his promotion to major general. His death brought about unprecedented grieving from the British populace, and in addition to his sunblocker, countless streets, towns, bays, and even an island were named for him in Britain, Canada, the United States, New Zealand, and Swaziland.

There is also a statue of Havelock in Trafalgar Square in London, paid for by public prescription in 1861.

Part of its plaque reads, "Soldiers! Your labours, your privations, your suffering and your valour, will not be forgotten by a grateful country." Perhaps ironically, in 2003 London's mayor, Ken Livingstone, unsuccessfully lobbied to have the statue and that of General Charles James Napier replaced with "more relevant" figures, saying, "I haven't got a clue who they are." Perhaps it would have heled if Havelock were wearing a hat.

⋖knickers⋗

n. pl. a short-legged (orig. knee-length), freq. loose-fitting, pair of pants worn by women and children as an undergarment

—*Oxford English Dictionary*

The word *knickers* comes from the leggings worn by the fictional Diedrich Knickerbocker, whose name was derived from the austere and very real Harmen Knickerbocker. Suffice it to say that many members of the Knickerbocker lineage in New York have had their knickers in a twist over this for the last two hundred years.

Harmen Knickerbocker was the clan patriarch of a prominent social and political family in upstate New York in the early 1800s. He was friends with the legendary writer and historian Washington Irving, who used "Knickerbocker" as a pseudonym for his creation of a crotchety Dutch historian.

Irving is most famous for his short stories "The Legend of Sleepy Hollow" and "Rip Van Winkle," but it was his 1809 satire *A History of New-York from the Beginning of the World to the End of the Dutch Dynasty* that made its fictional author—Diedrich Knickerbocker—a household name. Irving's mockery of inflated local history and small-minded politics was a huge success, and the name Knickerbocker eventually became a nickname for anyone living in Manhattan (shortened to Knicks for those who merely play basketball there).

Eventually, an English edition of the book featured illustrations by the classic Charles Dickens illustrator George Cruikshank, who drew the fictitious and stodgy Knickerbocker family in loose, knee-length Dutch breeches. Over the next few decades, the short and loose ladies' undergarments that became popular in England were dubbed "knickers."

Knickers aside, Washington Irving further lampooned New York's power brokers in a literary magazine called *Salmagundi* under the pseudonyms William Wizard and Launcelot Langstaff. It was here that he was the first to describe New York City as "Gotham," which is an Anglo-Saxon word meaning "Goat's Town." He was also the first to coin the phrase *almighty dollar*, in 1837's "The Creole Village," and it was a dream sequence in an 1812 revision of *A History of New York* that first featured old St. Nick cruising the Christmas skies in a flying wagon.

But to return to pantaloons, while knickers (and their twisting) became standard British slang for delicate unmentionables, baggy trousers for women in the United States in the nineteenth and early twentieth centuries were called "bloomers," named for early feminist Amelia Jenks Bloomer.

But that is another story.

⊰Beau Brummell⊱

n. a dandy or fop

—*Webster's New Universal Unabridged Dictionary,*
Second Edition

Any man requiring eight hours of primping time to prepare for a party and insisting on separate designers for the fingers, thumb, and palm of his gloves clearly deserves eternal castigation as a dandy.

If Madame de Pompadour was the stylish toast of France in the middle of the eighteenth century (see *pompadour*), then George Bryan Brummell was her British counterpoint at the end of it. Like Pompadour, Brummell was born of relatively modest means in 1778, the son of a secretary and grandson of a shopkeeper. He had the good fortune to be able to attend the exclusive boarding school at Eton and, later, Oriel College at Oxford. Already a preening fashionmonger, he rubbed elbows and curling irons with the greatest young aristocrats of the day—including the ever portly Prince of Wales, who would eventually become prince regent in 1811 and King(-sized) George IV in 1820 (his coronation waistline was fifty inches).

The monarch-to-be took a shine to the spectacularly witty and foppish Brummell and commissioned him to his own military regiment in 1794. Exhausted from his meteoric rise to captain (and blessed with a windfall inheritance), Brummell retired to a life of leisure in 1798, at the tender age of twenty. By all accounts, he was fanatically obsessed with his own appearance and spent nearly twenty years bankrolling countless tailors, jewelers, and haberdashers. His outfits were the talk of London, and his opinions were the final word on debates of fashion. Brummell allegedly once said, "Starch makes the gentleman, etiquette the lady" and "If people turn to look at you on the street, you are not well dressed." In addition to effectively inventing the modern gentleman's dress of a dark suit and knotted tie, he is rumored to have polished his boots with champagne and, in a country never noted for its dental hygiene, fastidiously brushed his teeth each day.

Unfortunately, Brummell also began gambling well beyond his means. His actual inheritance could not accommodate his lavish lifestyle or keep pace with his social circle of aristocrats. He also discovered that royal cliques are fickle mistresses, and Brummell's relations with the rotund regent began cooling a bit, culminating in an outright courtly cold shoulder in 1813. At one particular ball, the prince greeted his usual companions warmly but ignored Brummell, infamously leading the snubbed dandy to ask one of the retinue, "Who's your fat friend?" And so was bitten the hand that fed him. Brummell was still able to float loans for his debts from other wealthy friends, but only for three more years. He finally fled to France in 1816 to escape his creditors.

Brummell's twenty-four-year exile in France led to a short stint in a debtor's prison, ongoing battles with paralysis and venereal disease, and (ironically) a downward slide into wretched dress. He spent the last two years of his life in a charity insane asylum, dying in 1840 at the age of sixty-one. Yet he was not forgotten. Beyond his pejorative namesake, his flamboyant life has been dramatized in plays, operettas, and films, and his name has since been applied to watches, colognes, and business suits.

✦ argyle ✦

n. a geometric knitting pattern of varicolored diamonds in solid and outline shapes on a single background color; *also*: a sock knit in this pattern
—*Webster's New Universal Unabridged Dictionary,*
Second Edition

The Campbell clan of Argyll (Argyle) is among the most famous and powerful in Scotland's history. Today, we wear their socks.

Tartans are the stereotypically Scottish patterns of crisscrossed color blocks decorating the kilts that most people assume all Scots don before airing out a bagpipe tune or sidling up to a steaming plate of neeps and tatties. While it is equally easy to conjure up a historical tableau of kilted warriors marching across a heathered moor, the truth is that the diagnostic striped and checkered plaids did not exist in Scotland until the sixteenth century and were primarily used to distinguish regions and districts for two centuries before representing individual clans in the 1800s.

A somewhat artificial renaissance of tartans took place in 1822 when the fashion-conscious King George IV of England (see *Beau Brummell*) visited Scotland and was treated to a veritable pomp of plaid pageantry. Largely responsible for George's invitation and certainly central to the nation's historical resurgence was Scottish novelist Sir Walter Scott, who had founded the Celtic Society of Edinburgh two years prior and was already wildly popular for his multiple historical novels romanticizing Scotland's highlands and traditional dress. Following George's visit, many Scottish clans responded to this nationalistic furor by inventing their own tartans—among them the green and white, diagonal checkerboard pattern of the Campbell clan of Argyll.

The first Campbells appeared in Scotland in the late thirteenth century and became dominant in the western region of Argyll over the next three hundred years. Duncan Campbell became the first lord of Argyll in 1445, Colin Campbell the first earl of Argyll in 1457, and Archibald Campbell the first duke of Argyll in 1701. There have been twelve more dukes in the centuries since—all grand nobles of Scottish history and some featured prominently in Sir Walter Scott's *Rob Roy* and his *Tales of My Landlord* series. Soon after King George's visit, the green and white diamond tartan of the Campbell clan was co-opted by textile manufacturers as "argyle plaid" and led eventually to the multicolored argyle socks. Today there are thousands of different tartan designs, and hundreds of new ones are registered each year through the Scottish Tartans Authority or the Scottish Tartans World Register. But argyle is the most undeniably ubiquitous.

Still, it seems somewhat superficial to reduce the cultural contributions of this proud Scottish family to ankle apparel. Perhaps, instead, historical focus should spotlight the eighth duke of Argyll, who once sensitively noticed that his cattle and sheep were plagued with flies and biting insects. Legend has it that he decreed that all pastures should have scratching posts erected for the comfort of suffering grazers. To this day, itches satisfied with a lusty Scottish scratch are followed with the thankful exclamation, "God bless the Duke of Argyll!"

cardigan

n. a usu. collarless sweater or jacket that opens the full length of the center front

—*Merriam-Webster's Collegiate Dictionary, Eleventh Edition*

Cannon to right of them,
Cannon to left of them,
Cannon in front of them
Volley'd and thunder'd;
Storm'd at with shot and shell,
Boldly they rode and well,
Into the jaws of Death,
Into the mouth of hell
Rode the six hundred

. . . in cardigans. Alfred Tennyson's rousing retelling of the historic Charge of the Light Brigade is a poetic testament to the exploits of James Thomas Brudenell, the seventh earl of Cardigan, whose namesake knitwear unfortunately far surpasses his military legacy.

Brudenell was born in Buckinghamshire, England, in 1797 and inherited his father's earldom of Cardigan in Northamptonshire forty years later. Always an aristocrat, after entering the army, Brudenell capitalized on the then common British practice of selling military commissions to noblemen and purchased his own promotions to lieutenant, captain, major, and lieutenant colonel in five short years. He was much loathed by superiors and subordinates alike—thwarted in an attempt to court-martial one of his soldiers and deemed "unfit to command" by his senior officer—and was apparently no more charming in his personal life. He endured an unhappy marriage of twenty years before eventually separating from his wife and indulging in a notorious affair while his wife was on her deathbed.

He eventually became a lieutenant general and in

1854 was placed in charge of the Light Cavalry Brigade during the Battle of Balaclava of the Crimean War. While a cavalcade of finger-pointing followed the attack, a small handful of details seems to be agreed on. While English, French, and Turkish forces were trying to capture Russia's primary naval base on the Black Sea and orders were given to retrieve several captured British guns, Brudenell's six hundred mounted troops were mistakenly directed (under protest) to charge blindly through Balaclava's North Valley under the sweltering hellfire of Russian guns and marksmen. Upon heroically and inconceivably reaching the end of the valley and realizing a catastrophic error had been made, the brigade retreated back through the heavy fire. Roughly one hundred troops were killed, though Brudenell survived unscathed. Despite spending most of the war aboard his steam yacht in Balaclava's harbor and failing to keep his troops properly supplied, Brudenell returned to England a hero, (self-)proclaiming his great valor. Subsequent reports eventually maintained that Brudenell might never have actually engaged the enemy, but the general never retracted his claims. He died after falling from a horse in 1868.

What has since brought Brudenell sartorial infamy, however, is the stylish woolen vest he wore to protect himself from the bracing elements of the Russian winter in Crimea (see *Potemkin*). Brudenell insisted that all of his officers be flamboyantly dressed, and he led the charge in splendid regalia. His knitted waistcoat was soon embraced by clothiers hoping to capitalize on his widespread popularity and eventually morphed into the collarless V-neck sweater embraced by such pacifists as children's television luminary "Mister" Fred Rogers.

Pierre François Joseph Bosquet was a French commander who witnessed the Charge of the Light Brigade, and it is difficult to know whether he was referring to the battle tactics or the Earl of Cardigan's fuzzy sweater vest when he famously observed, "It is magnificent, but it is not war. It is madness."

⊰ sideburns ⊱

n. short whiskers grown only on the cheeks
—*Webster's New Universal Unabridged Dictionary,*
Second Edition

Though they enjoy a popular counterculture resurgence every few decades (and remain a fashion mainstay for particular niches of the entertainment industry), the golden age of sideburns was unquestionably the American Civil War—led by the hirsute charge of Ambrose Burnside, who will long be remembered not for his positions as general, governor, senator, or even president of the National Rifle Association but for his outrageous facial hair.

Burnside was born in Indiana in 1824 and graduated

from the U.S. Military Academy in 1843. He guarded garrisons in the Mexican-American War, protected western mail routes as part of the U.S. cavalry, and received an Apache arrow in the neck before first leaving the army in 1853. He remained in the Rhode Island militia, however, and manufactured his namesake Burnside carbine rifle until he was forced to sell his patent after his factory burned down and he lost an expensive congressional race.

The outbreak of the Civil War seemed to give him a second chance, and rising up from his position as a brigadier general in the Rhode Island militia, he commanded an entire brigade at the First Battle of Bull Run. Despite his acknowledged lack of military experience and his repeated insistence to Abraham Lincoln that he was not qualified for the job, Burnside was eventually appointed to succeed General George B. McClellan as commander of the Army of the Potomac. However, after disastrous defeats at the Battle of Fredericksburg and later the Battle of the Crater in Petersburg, Burnside finally decided to resign.

Widely regarded in retrospect as being unfit for high command, Burnside is nonetheless remembered as an extraordinarily nice guy. He shook enough hands and slapped enough backs to become a railroad mogul, a governor and U.S. senator of Rhode Island, and the very first president of the NRA. But it was his signature facial hair—flamboyant muttonchops conjoined by a hearty mustache with a clean-shaven chin—that gave him infamy. His "burnsides" eventually flipped syllables to give us our sideburns of today.

Sideburns have varied in length, shape, and name in subsequent years. They are called "side-whiskers" or "sideboards" in the United Kingdom. They have spanned the social map from presidents (most notably Chester Arthur and Martin Van Buren) to actors (James Dean) to singers (Elvis Presley) to football players (Joe Namath). There are "muttonchops" (flaring out across the jawline) and "friendly muttonchops" (connected with a mustache). There is even a special category for them in the biannual World Beard and Moustache Championships. A hairless chin remains sacrosanct, however, lest the jowls be joined to form a beard.

Among the most spectacular sideburns of history were the jawline drapes sported by Edward Sothern in his portrayal of the eccentric and dim-witted Lord Dundreary in Tom Taylor's play *Our American Cousin* (later made extraordinarily famous for being the featured entertainment the night Abraham Lincoln was shot). Sothern's sweeping facial locks eventually merited their own name (see *dundrearies*).

But the original hipster, Ambrose Burnside, died in 1881. He was quickly immortalized in stone, and he and his boundless whiskers, astride his noble steed, are now permanent residents in Burnside Park in Providence, Rhode Island.

❧ dundrearies ❧

n. long flowing sideburns

—*Merriam-Webster's Collegiate Dictionary, Eleventh Edition*

Perhaps no one has ever carried facial hair to such Rapunzelesque lengths (see *sideburns*) as Edward Askew Sothern did in the late 1850s for the foppish character of Lord Dundreary in Tom Taylor's comic play *Our American Cousin*. Though they were sometimes referred to as "Piccadilly weepers" or "Newgate knockers," it is unclear why his unusual sideburns came to be called "dundrearies" instead of adopting the name of their creator. Perhaps it was felt that calling them "sotherns" during the height of the American Civil War would have needlessly prolonged the duration of the conflict.

Sothern was an English actor, born in Liverpool in 1826. His first professional acting gig was in 1849 in *Lady of Lyons* by Edward Bulwer-Lytton (whose now infamous story opener "It was a dark and stormy night" provides the basis for the annual Bulwer-Lytton Fiction Contest for bad writing). Eventually moving to America and wanting to be regarded as a serious actor, Sothern was somewhat hesitant to take on the supporting role of the weak-minded aristocrat Lord Dundreary in *Our American Cousin*. However, soon after the comedy premiered in New York in 1858, Sothern came to own the role and began ad-libbing and injecting exaggerated mannerisms into his performance, which made him a sensation in the United States and in England.

A key element of his comedic presence was his flowing whiskers, which drooped down to his shoulders—a style that would eventually bear his character's name. Sothern's performance also helped coin another short-lived term—*dundrearyisms*—for his nonsensical combinations of colloquial phrases. Lord Dundreary famously remarked that "Birds of a feather gather no moss." Sothern's characterization was so popular that it spawned a number of sequels, including *Dundreary Married and Done For* and *Our American Cousin at Home, or Lord Dundreary Abroad.*

The original *Our American Cousin* was the play being performed at Ford's Theatre in Washington, DC, the night Abraham Lincoln was shot. John Wilkes Booth used as cover the riotous laughter following the line "You sockdologizing old man-trap!" to shoot the president.

Sothern himself died in 1881, at the age of fifty-four. A notorious prankster his entire life, his funeral was largely unattended because so many of his friends and family assumed it was a hoax.

⊰ leotard ⊱

n. a close-fitting one-piece garment worn by acrobats and dancers

—*Oxford English Dictionary*

Our word for the classic (and revealing) uniform of ballerinas and gymnasts is the namesake of Jules Léotard, a vainglorious French acrobat who wanted nothing more than female adoration of what he considered his "best features."

Perhaps the directors of the 1984 Val Kilmer comedy *Top Secret!* had Léotard in mind when they featured a ballerina gracefully leaping from loin to loin in a gauntlet of male dancers, resting each time on their ridiculously exaggerated accoutrement, to an appropriately chosen accompaniment from *The Nutcracker.*

Jules Léotard was born to circus performer parents in Toulouse, France, in the middle of the nineteenth century. Though originally on track to become a lawyer, he became enamored with the trapeze bars (and, apparently, his own physique) and joined the Cirque Napoleon in 1859. Donning his invention, what he called a *maillot*—a skin-tight, one-piece garment with long sleeves to allow free movement and to display his muscles—Léotard became the first trapeze artist to execute a midair somersault and the first to swing from one trapeze to another. All of this was in the days before safety nets (introduced in 1871). Léotard often performed over a stack of mattresses or, more often, directly over the heads of diners in music halls.

So impressive were his flights and flips that in 1867 he was the direct inspiration for what has become the anthem of aerial acrobats—"The Daring Young Man on the Flying Trapeze."

> *The girl that I loved she was handsome,*
> *I tried all I knew her to please,*
> *But I could not please her one quarter so well*

As that man upon the trapeze.
He'd fly thro' the air with the greatest of ease—
A daring young man on the flying trapeze—
His movements were graceful, all girls he could please,
And my love he purloined away.

Léotard's word *maillot* is now used for jerseys or swimsuits, having been replaced by *leotard* in 1886, nearly twenty years after the acrobat's premature death, from smallpox, before his thirtieth birthday. The design was certainly created for men, and Léotard was quite explicit about the effect he hoped his invention would have, as he describes in his *Memoires*:

"Do you want to be adored by the ladies? [I]nstead of draping yourself in unflattering clothes, invented by ladies . . . put on a more natural garb, which does not hide your best features."

•TAWDRY CALENDAR•

JANUARY

7—Death of André Maginot (1932), *Maginot*

11—Death of Georges-Eugène Haussmann (1891), *Haussmannize*

12—Birth of James Henry Salisbury (1823), *Salisbury steak*

18—Death of Charles Ponzi (1949), *Ponzi scheme*

21—Death of Edward Askew "Lord Dundreary" Sothern (1881), *dundrearies*

27—Birth of Leopold von Sacher-Masoch (1836), *masochism*

27—Death of Thomas Crapper (1910), *crapper*

28—Execution of William Burke (1829), *burke*

30—Death of Harmen Knickerbocker (1855), *knickers*

31—Death of Ernesto Arturo Miranda (1976), *Miranda (warning and rights)*

FEBRUARY

10—Death of Joseph Lister (1910), *Listerine*

12—Death of Astley Cooper (1841), *Cooper's ligaments*

17—Birth of André Maginot (1877), *Maginot*

23—Death of Nellie Melba (1931), *Melba toast*

24—Death of Thomas Bowdler (1825), *bowdlerize*

26—Death of Richard Jordan Gatling (1903), *Gatling gun*

Exact date unknown—Birth of Epicurus (341 BC), *epicure*

Exact date unknown—Death of Osman I (1326), *ottoman*

MARCH

2—Birth of Samuel Houston (1793), *Houstonize*

3—Birth of Charles Ponzi (1882), *Ponzi scheme*

5—Death of Franz Anton Mesmer (1815), *mesmerize*

7—Birth of Anthony Comstock (1844), *Comstockery*

9—Birth of Vyacheslav Molotov (1890), *Molotov cocktail*

9—Death of Leopold von Sacher-Masoch (1895), *masochism*

9—Birth of Ernesto Arturo Miranda (1941), *Miranda* (*warning and rights*)

9—Debut of Barbie (1959), *Barbie*

12—Birth of Charles Cunningham Boycott (1832), *boycott*

13—Death of Henry Shrapnel (1842), *shrapnel*

16—Death of William Banting (1878), *Bantingism*

26—Death of Joseph-Ignace Guillotin (1814), *guillotine*

27—Birth of Georges-Eugène Haussmann (1809), *Haussmannize*

28—Death of James Thomas Brudenell, seventh earl of Cardigan (1868), *cardigan*

29—Birth of Bertha Krupp von Bohlen und Halbach (1886), *Big Bertha*

30—Death of Beau Brummell (1840), *Beau Brummell*

APRIL

1—Birth of Edward Askew "Lord Dundreary" Sothern (1826), *dundrearies*

2—Birth of Giacomo Casanova de Seingalt (1725), *Casanova*

5—Birth of Henry Havelock (1795), *havelock*

5—Birth of Joseph Lister (1827), *Listerine*

7—Birth of Charles Fourier (1772), *Fourierism*

15—Death of Madame de Pompadour (1764), *pompadour*

25—Birth of Oliver Cromwell (1599), *Oliver's skull*

Exact date unknown—Birth of Fanny Adams (1859), *Fanny Adams*

MAY

2—Death of Joseph McCarthy (1957), *McCarthyism*

3—Birth of Niccolò dei Machiavelli (1469), *Machiavellian*

4—Death of Jean Nicot de Villemain (1600), *nicotine*

10—Birth of James Gordon Bennett Jr. (1841), *Gordon Bennett!*

14—Death of James Gordon Bennett Jr. (1918), *Gordon Bennett!*

19—Birth of Nellie Melba (1861), *Melba toast*

23—Birth of Franz Anton Mesmer (1734), *mesmerize*

23—Birth of Ambrose Burnside (1824), *sideburns*

28—Birth of Joseph-Ignace Guillotin (1738), *guillotine*

31—Death of Joachim Neander (1680), *Neanderthal*

JUNE

2—Birth of the Marquis de Sade (1740), *sadism*

3—Birth of Henry Shrapnel (1761), *shrapnel*

4—Death of Giacomo Casanova de Seingalt (1798), *Casanova*

7—Death of Louise de La Vallière (1710), *lavaliere*

7—Birth of Beau Brummell (1778), *Beau Brummell*

15—Death of Henry Sacheverell (1724), *sacheverell*

19—Death of Charles Cunningham Boycott (1897), *boycott*

20—Birth of Errol Flynn (1909), *in like Flynn*

21—Death of Niccolò dei Machiavelli (1527), *Machiavellian*

21—Death of John Thompson (1940), *tommy gun*

23—Death of Titus Flavius Vespasianus (79), *vespasienne*

23—Feast day of St. Audrey, *tawdry*

28—Death of the Duchess de Fontanges (1681), *fontange*

JULY

4—Birth of Reuben Goldberg (1883), *Rube Goldberg*

5—Birth of Sylvester Graham (1794), *graham cracker*

11—Birth of Thomas Bowdler (1754), *bowdlerize*

17—Birth of Elbridge Gerry (1744), *gerrymander*

18—Birth of Vidkun Quisling (1887), *quisling*

22—Birth of William Archibald Spooner (1844), *spoonerism*

23—Steve Brodie allegedly jumps off the Brooklyn Bridge (1886), *brodie*

26—Death of Samuel Houston (1863), *Houstonize*

27—Birth of Harmen Knickerbocker (1779), *knickers*

AUGUST

6—Birth of Louise de La Vallière (1644), *lavaliere*

7—Birth of Margaretha Geertruida Zelle (1876), *Mata Hari*

17—Birth of Mae West (1893), *Mae West*

23—Birth of Astley Cooper (1768), *Cooper's ligaments*

24—Death of Fanny Adams (1867), *Fanny Adams*

29—Death of William Archibald Spooner (1930), *spoonerism*

SEPTEMBER

11—Death of Sylvester Graham (1851), *graham cracker*

12—Birth of Richard Jordan Gatling (1818), *Gatling gun*

13—Death of Ambrose Burnside (1881), *sideburns*

21—Death of Anthony Comstock (1915), *Comstockery*

21—Death of Bertha Krupp von Bohlen und Halbach (1957), *Big Bertha*

23—Death of Oliver Cromwell (1658), *Oliver's skull*

23—Birth of Mary Mallon (1869), *Typhoid Mary*

23—Death of James Henry Salisbury (1905), *Salisbury steak*

24—Birth of Grigory Potemkin (1739), *Potemkin*

OCTOBER

10—Death of Charles Fourier (1837), *Fourierism*

14—Death of Errol Flynn (1959), *in like Flynn*

15—Death of Margaretha Geertruida Zelle (1917), *Mata Hari*

16—Death of Grigory Potemkin (1791), *Potemkin*

16—Birth of James Thomas Brudenell, seventh earl of Cardigan (1797), *cardigan*

17—St. Audrey's Day celebrated, *tawdry*

21—Birth of Alfred Nobel (1833), *Nobel Prize*

24—Death of Vidkun Quisling (1945), *quisling*

29—Death of Charles Lynch (1796), *lynch*

30—Death of Edward "Old Grog" Vernon (1757), *grog*

Exact date unknown—Assassination of Philip II of Macedon (336 BC), *philippic*

NOVEMBER

4—Birth of Joseph McCarthy (1908), *McCarthyism*

8—Death of Vyacheslav Molotov (1986), *Molotov cocktail*

10—Birth of Mikhail Kalashnikov (1919), *AK-47*

11—Death of Mary Mallon (1938), *Typhoid Mary*

12—Birth of Edward "Old Grog" Vernon (1684), *grog*

12—First public appearance of Jules Léotard (1859), *leotard*

17—Birth of Titus Flavius Vespasianus (9), *vespasienne*

18—Death of Christopher Pinchbeck (1732), *pinchbeck*

22—Death of Mae West (1980), *Mae West*

23—Death of Elbridge Gerry (1814), *gerrymander*

25—Feast day of St. Catherine of Alexandria, *Catherine wheel*
29—Death of Henry Havelock (1857), *havelock*
29—Death of Peter Rachman (1962), *Rachmanism*

DECEMBER
2—Death of the Marquis de Sade (1814), *sadism*
5—Execution of John Bishop (1831), *bishop*
7—Death of Reuben Goldberg (1970), *Rube Goldberg*
8—Death of John Duns Scotus (1308), *dunce*
10—Death of Alfred Nobel (1896), *Nobel Prize*
29—Birth of Madame de Pompadour (1721), *pompadour*
31—Birth of John Thompson (1860), *tommy gun*

· A C K N O W L E D G M E N T S ·

Without the help of these individuals, this book would still have been entirely possible. But I would like to thank them anyway for their input, support, and fellowship:

Patrick "I So Wanted Scofflaw to Be a Real Person" Alexander; Jeff "Velvet Kenny Rogers" Beebe; Mia "Bombshell" Bloom; Hester "It's Not Gibberish; It's . . . Latin" Blum; Edwin "High Tea at the Four Seasons" Buckhalter; Jerry "Moonshine" and Michele "Crack Shot" Calistri; Stephanie "Chilympian" Cobb; Amy "I Could Imagine Buying This Book" Downey; Jonathan "Praise-God Barebones" Eburne; Allan "Conan the Grammarian" Fallow; Rachel "The Guillotine Song" Graham; Schuyler "The Greeks Do Love Their Analogies" Hibbard; John "Said the Actress to the Bishop" Horgan; Karen "Living the Dream" Kostyal; David "Sequel? Stormy Petrel: Unfortunate Definitions Associated with Animals" Levin; Lisa "Don't You Worry Your Pretty Little Head" Lytton; Josh "Hot Yogurt" Moline; Tony "Boots" Mulliken; Billie Jo "Bocker" and Patrick "One Hundred and One Is as Alliterative as Ninety" North; Larry "Halcyon Days" Porges; Ned "The Man Behind the Man" Rust; April "Pistol-Packin'" Scimio; Tony "Tonti Was an Italian Baker" Shugaar; Julie "Case of Wine in the Overhead Compartment" Simpson; William "Cromwell Is a Very Prominent Historical and Psychological Demon" and Sharon "Dear Folks" Simpson; Jamie "Not a Dancing Ham" Taylor; John "Merkle Was the First Bonehead" and Megan "Hello, Santa?" Tooker; Andrés "Patsy? Is Patsy One?" Villalta; and Jason "Welcome to New York" Woodruff

My parents: Miriam "Five Languages and Counting" and Gregor "More People Would Read This If It Were Written in Chinese" Novak

My copyeditor: Sheila "Potty Mouth" Moody

My editor: Jeanette "The Author Has Such a Lively Writing Style and His Fascination with Words Shines Through on Each Page" Shaw

My deus ex machina: Luke "This One's Dangling" Anderson

My agent and her boss: Erin "I've Given Up Champagne for Lent" Niumata and Jeff "We Believe in Carrying Concealed Firearms around the Office" Kleinman

My inspiration and the finest writer, instructor, and gentleman I have known: Robert "Carnie, Pimp, and Snake Charmer" Coram

And, most important, my saucy and spirited wife, partner, and favorite publishing expat: Katie "You Do Know That Knickers Are Underwear, Right?" Novak

·INDEX·

·ABOUT THE AUTHOR·

Alex Novak has always loved words and was a spectacular nerd as a child. He has been an editor with the National Geographic Society, Time Warner, and the Explorers Club in New York City. He plays bluegrass guitar and man-dolin, juggles machetes, rides a unicycle, and spits fire. He is equally comfortable discussing *The Simpsons* and the stylistic differences between the fourteenth and fifteenth editions of *The Chicago Manual of Style*.

He received an M.A. in journalism from Indiana Univer-sity, received a B.A. in English and a B.S. in anthropology and human biology from Emory University, and has served as an adjunct professor of journalism at Penn State Univer-sity. He is currently the executive director of the Interna-tional Center for the Study of Terrorism.

He now lives in a Victorian home in central Pennsylva-nia with his wife and daughter, two hives of bees, a giant English mastiff named Chester, and a rotary phone (see *Luddite*).